The *Way* of the

Hedge
Witch

RITUALS AND SPELLS FOR
HEARTH AND HOME

Arin Murphy-Hiscock

PROVENANCE
PRESS

Adams Media
Avon, Massachusetts

Copyright © 2009 by F+W Media, Inc.
All rights reserved. This book, or parts thereof, may not be reproduced in any
form without permission from the publisher; exceptions are made for brief
excerpts used in published reviews.

Published by
Provenance Press®,
an imprint of Adams Media, a division of F+W Media, Inc.
57 Littlefield Street
Avon, MA 02322
www.adamsmedia.com
Provenance Press® is a registered trademark of F+W Media, Inc.

ISBN-10: 1-59869-974-1
ISBN-13: 978-1-59869-974-6

Printed in the United States of America.

J I H G F E D C B A

Library of Congress Cataloging-in-Publication Data
is available from the publisher.

This publication is designed to provide accurate and authoritative information
with regard to the subject matter covered. It is sold with the understanding that
the publisher is not engaged in rendering legal, accounting, or other professional advice. If legal advice or other expert assistance is required, the services
of a competent professional person should be sought.
—From a *Declaration of Principles* jointly adopted by a Committee of the
American Bar Association and a Committee of Publishers and Associations

Many of the designations used by manufacturers and sellers to distinguish their
product are claimed as trademarks. Where those designations appear in this
book and Adams Media was aware of a trademark claim, the designations have
been printed with initial capital letters.

Interior illustration by Elisabeth Lariviere.

*This book is available at quantity discounts for bulk purchases.
For information, please call 1-800-289-0963.*

Contents

Dedication

This one is for the chosen family, with specific nods to:

Pasley, Jeff, Devon, and Tallis

Janice and Taras

Ceri and Scott

Daphné

Acknowledgments

It's appropriate that this book focuses on family and home-based spirituality, because family and chosen family were key in my life as I wrote it.

A hearty hurrah goes out to Janice for her support throughout this book. Not only did she allow me to use her easy bread recipe, she came over every Friday to work on her own manuscript in the kitchen, cheered me along the way, and kept me focused. Ceri, Pasley, Rob, Daphné, Lu, Rosy, Bodhifox and the rest of the regulars gave me ongoing encouragement that I really needed during this project while I struggled with the development of fibromyalgia and had to drastically reassess my work habits and schedule. And thank you to Miranda for being the best caregiver a little boy could ask for. Thanks also go out to everyone who said, "Hearthcraft sounds intriguing, what does it mean?" and was patient when I didn't answer them because I either couldn't put it into words at the time, or forgot about the question because I was busy with the book.

Andrea Norville at Provenance Press® was an enthusiastic supporter when I took her original idea of cauldron-focused magic and spun it into something completely different, and cheerfully gave me an extension when I asked for one. The anonymous copyeditors and proofreaders have my undying thanks as well for their help.

Love, as always, to Ron and Liam, who had to deal with meals and home maintenance on their own more than I'd like to admit because I lost track of time as I worked.

Introduction

Hearth and Home

Many people follow a home-based spiritual path that can't be clearly defined or identified as an existing Neo-Pagan path. *Hedge witch* is one term that is sometimes encountered when reading about followers of paths such as this. In some circles it has the connotation of one who engages in traditional shamanic practice involving spirit journeys or trancing, often with the aid and support of herbal knowledge. In other circles it is another term for a solitary nature-based spiritual path. Wise women, cunning men, and other such practitioners were sometimes called green witches or hedge witches, and they worked to heal individuals, communities, and any malaise in the natural world. Very often they worked out of their own homes, making those homes repositories and sources of healing energy and knowledge, both collected and crafted.

A hedge borders properties, separating private land from public land and order from chaos, and this is one of the main themes of this book. The hedge is more than a physical barrier: it is a symbol of spiritual protection from the stresses of the outside world. Inside this protective enclosure you can create a rejuvenating environment, one that is spiritually supportive and nourishing. In traditional shamanic practice the hedge is perceived as a barrier between the world of men and the realm of the spiritual world, a boundary to be crossed while in shamanic trance in search of solutions and information. Whereas shamanic work is a fascinating subject and worthy of study, it isn't what I've chosen to focus on in this book. Instead, it explores the home and hearth as representative of valuable knowledge and energy that can be used to deepen and enrich your spiritual path, whatever that may be.

Like *The Way of the Green Witch*, this book seeks to help you develop your own home-based spiritual practice. While *The Way of the Green Witch* focused on using the energies of the natural world to support your spiritual practice, *The Way of the Hedge Witch* explores the energies of hearth and home and how they can enrich your spiritual work and life. I've chosen to focus on the concept of hearth and home throughout this book because it's a concept that is often overlooked in books about solitary nature-based practices. Solitary alternative spiritual paths often look beyond the home to what lies outside it to focus on the natural world. Creating a solid and supportive place to work from both spiritually and in everyday life—a literal home base—is a step many people don't think to take.

The home is the center of power for an individual and family. It is a place of refuge, renewal, and creativity, where we begin and end each day. It is a place where we are nourished, rested, and otherwise strengthened. The home reflects the individuals who live within it on several levels, including a physical level (choice of décor and arrangement) and spiritual level (the energy or "feel" of a home). The home is the primary root of your family's energy and spirituality. If you work to honor and strengthen that center of power and renewal, making it as peaceful and spiritually nourishing as possible for you and your family, then you are working to create and maintain a place of peace and a source of energy.

The concept of the home as spiritual center is found in many cultures and throughout many eras. The home, and in particular the hearth, has often served as a point of connection for gods and humankind. Many people today seek some sort of practice through which they can empower their homes to serve as part of their spiritual philosophy. There is little existing literature on the subject of modern hearth-based spiritual practice and magic, an oversight that this book seeks to correct.

This book explores the idea of home-based spirituality using two symbols as joint keystones: the cauldron, and the flame. The cauldron is a traditional representation of abundance and hospitality. It is also a symbol of rebirth, mystery, creation, and transformation, making it the perfect symbol to use as a focus in hearth and home-based spirituality. The flame is a symbol of life, activity, the Divine, purification, and creativity, making it an excellent partner for the cauldron.

The Way of the Hedge Witch is written for the Pagan or Pagan-friendly reader seeking a free-form practice centered in the home and family, and offers a thoughtful look at creating a haven and refuge to spiritually nurture families in today's busy world. Focusing on everyday living and uncomplicated practice with simple hearth-based rituals throughout, this book outlines a safe, comforting, and empowering path for the modern practitioner seeking to root him- or herself in the heart of their own lives, exploring ways to recognize the commonplace as spiritual.

In essence, the role of the hearth-based hedge witch is to serve as a facilitator for spiritual well-being of herself, her family, and her welcomed guests. Her home is her temple, which she tends in order to keep energy flowing smoothly and freely, as well as to honor the principles she upholds. She seeks to support, nurture, and nourish her family (and extended community) in both a spiritual and physical fashion. This book will help you to explore spiritual connections that may be found or created in the home.

Before you read on, you may wish to think about these questions:

+ What constitutes the spiritual element of home-based activity?
+ How do you seek and find a spiritual dimension to everyday activity?
+ How do you actively and deliberately assign a spiritual dimension to everyday activity?

Note: As in my previous books, this path is equally followed and practiced by both men and women. As those who tend the hearth physically and spiritually still tend to be women in Western culture, both traditionally and in contemporary life, this book presents itself to a female reader. There is nothing that is gender-specific, however, and everything within the book is equally applicable to and practiced by men. Women do not have an exclusive claim to being spiritual guardians of the home, or being those who tend the hearth in any of its forms. The path of the nurturer and spiritual guide for the family is equally open to men and women.

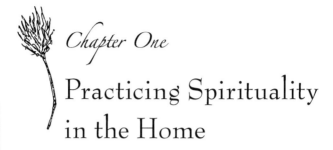

Chapter One

Practicing Spirituality in the Home

If there's something we all have in common, it's the need for shelter and nourishment, and for a place we call home. That place is somewhere to which we return for refuge, renewal, rest, relaxation, and rejuvenation.

The individual who practices a hearth and home-based magic walks one of the most ancient and simple of paths. Rooted in family and everyday life, the hearth-based hedge witch uses common objects and activity to nourish her spirituality. This book explores the concept of the home, and its central place in the spiritual life of the family. Spirituality comes from within; the spiritual path or practice we choose to engage in is a method of giving it context. One of the most common of those contexts is the hearth, the spiritual center of the home. No matter what your current spiritual path, organized or free-form and nebulous, rooting your spirituality in your hearth makes a lot of sense, and can and will nourish the rest of your spiritual life.

There are some basic concepts that drive this book and my definition of hearthcraft. It's important to address them right away, so you don't go through the book wondering what on earth I mean by the term. *Hearthcraft* is the term I use to describe the home-based portion of the spirituality associated with the path of the hedge witch. It is not kitchen witchcraft, although that can play a role within a hearth-focused hedge witch's practice. It is not green witchcraft, although that too can influence and enrich a hearth and home-based practice. Rather, it is a spiritual path rooted in the belief that the home is a place of beauty, power, and protection, a place where people are nurtured and nourished on a spiritual basis as well as a physical and emotional basis.

Although hearthcraft can be practiced by anyone of any defined religious path, this book is primarily aimed toward those of a Neo-Pagan bent, and the exercises and illustrations point to this fact. However, much of the information and work inside these pages are easily modified to reflect the beliefs of someone operating within a specific organized religion.

Hearthcraft argues that spirituality, like many other things, begins at home. It is not enough to attend an out-of-home spiritual gathering at specific intervals; the home itself is an essential element within a nourishing, vibrant, ongoing spiritual practice. Once upon a time organized religion was depended upon to be the source for spiritual fulfillment. With increasing dissatisfaction being felt within organized religious institutions, the relocation of the spiritual focus to the home, either as the central element or a supportive one, makes sense. Honoring the hearth means honoring your origins, where you come from each day, and where you return each night.

Why Hearthcraft?

Why have I come up with a new term when the term hedge witch is already out there? I consider the home-focused portion of the hedge witch's path worthy of its own focus and descriptive term.

The word "hearth" is of old English origin meaning the floor around a fireplace, or the lower part of a furnace where molten metal is collected during the smelting process. Throughout the ages the hearth has come to symbolize domestic comfort and the entire home, perceived as the heart or center of the living space. Therefore, someone who practices hearthcraft is someone whose spiritual practices revolve around the hearth and home, as symbolized by the fireplace and the fire that burns within it.

What about Kitchen Witches?

Perhaps a more familiar term, kitchen witch is used popularly to mean someone who practices magic through cooking, baking, and/or through everyday activity. Hearthcraft differentiates from kitchen witchcraft by primarily emphasizing the spiritual aspect that runs through the practice, as opposed to the primarily magical practice of the kitchen witch. There's more about kitchen witches later in this chapter.

Hearthcraft, like other aspects of the hedge witch's path and other forms of kitchen and green witchcraft, revolves around practicality, with little ritualistic guideline or necessary formality. Here's a list of some keywords to keep in mind when you think about hearthcraft:

- Simple
- Practical
- Family-related
- Domestic
- Everyday
- Household

The practices suggested in this book are based in simplicity. Here the word "ritual" doesn't mean something full-blown and complicated; instead, it means an intuitive ceremony or something set apart from everyday action by mindfulness and conscious intent. Also, the word "magic" means the conscious and directed attempt to effect change by combining and directing energy toward a positive goal. The rituals and magical workings included in this book are only guidelines to give you an idea of how you can structure your own hearth-based spiritual practice.

Spirituality in the Home

Hearthcraft functions on a very basic truth: The very living of your life is a spiritual act.

Having said that, it can be hard to isolate exactly what constitutes spirituality, and by extension, how to actively support it in the home.

The *Oxford Dictionary* primarily defines "spiritual" as "relating to or affecting the human spirit as opposed to material or physical things."

What makes hearthcraft so special is that the principles of it dovetail—in fact, are—the things you do every day in your home. In essence, this book is designed to help you recognize those things, and lend awareness to them so that you can appreciate them all the more. It also offers some ideas on how to enhance those everyday actions and objects, in order to facilitate or deepen your experience.

Nurturing the spiritual element of the home is key to the path of the hearth-based hedge witch. How can you do this? The answer depends on how you define "spiritual." I've already provided some basic definitions, but what is crucial to this practice is defining the term for yourself.

+ What constitutes a spiritual experience for you?
+ What are the characteristics of a sacred object?
+ What elements of an action render it spiritual?

These are huge questions, and the answers will be different for every person who tries to answer them. Attempting to define "spiritual" can be challenging, frustrating, and faith-testing. You may not be able to say more than, "I just know when something is spiritual," and that's fine. In essence, when we recognize something as spiritual, we acknowledge that something about it moves us or touches us deeply in a very specific way, evoking certain feelings that may be indefinable.

Once you know what kinds of things you find spiritual, or what kinds of events or actions evoke that response within yourself, then you may have some idea of where to focus in your practice of home-based spirituality, and how to identify or establish everyday activities that can support your spirituality, recognizing and using these spiritual moments to reinforce your commitment to making the home a spiritual place. One method of doing this is to use these moments or activities as an opportunity to think about "important" things (not important as in balancing your checkbook or picking up groceries for dinner, but about an issue related to your spirituality); an opportunity to send good thoughts out toward your family, friends, and community; an opportunity to practice a form of "walking meditation," where you perform a simple ongoing action with a clear mind; a moment to say a prayer, or simply open your heart and talk to God in whatever form you envision the Divine, the universe, the spirit of love, or whoever you feel like talking to.

Maintaining healthy spirituality means keeping yourself relaxed, focused, and practicing *something*. It means keeping the lines of communication open between you and something greater than you. The term "practice" is often used to describe what one does in respect to one's spiritual path, and it means physically or intentionally acting upon a theory associated with the path. By actively seeking out or defining spiritual activity, you create the opportunity to develop a deeper connection with the world around you.

Chapter 2 explores sanctity in more depth, especially as it pertains to the home.

The Magic of Everyday Activity

When the word "magic" is used one immediately suspects that things can no longer be practical or simple. The opposite is true, thankfully, particularly where hearthcraft is concerned!

There is always a sense that something that is simple cannot possibly be as effective or powerful or useful as something more complicated or difficult. This is an odd human perception. We love to complicate things for ourselves, possibly in order to have a scapegoat available if we fail. "It was too difficult!" we can cry. Humankind seems to instinctively eschew responsibility. But taking responsibility for your spiritual practice, working from the heart of your home outwards, is a step toward a more rewarding relationship with the world around you.

Everything is, or can be, a magical act. Stirring a pot of soup as you reheat it can be a magical act. So can wiping down the counter, washing the dishes, filling the kettle, and arranging your tea caddy. So how do you make these things magical? Not with secret words or arcane shapes drawn in the air. It isn't the *addition* of something that is necessary, so much as a *recognition* and acknowledgement of something that is already there.

What is necessary to enable such a recognition?

+ **Live in the moment.** Being in the moment is harder to do than it sounds. It means not thinking about your next action or the one you just performed, not thinking about how you have to leave in half an hour to pick the kids up from practice or how you have to remember to buy milk on the way home. It means thinking about what you are doing this precise moment instead. Just be. Feel the weight of the jug in your hand; feel the weight shift as you tilt it to pour the milk; hear the sound of the liquid flowing into the glass.
+ **Be aware of your intent.** Awareness is key to most magical working. While you are performing your action, make sure you have a clear expectation of the associated result or energy. Envisioning a clearly defined result is key to success.

- ✦ **Direct your energy properly.** Focus your will and allow it to fill the action you are performing. Poorly directed energy is wasted.
- ✦ **Focus on an action.** It may go without saying that there should be an action upon which to hang your magical work, but for the sake of clarity it's worth noting that a single action is better to focus on than a series of actions. It is harder to maintain focus over a long period of time, especially if you must change actions along the way.

Remember, hearthcraft is about keeping things simple and focused on the actual work you are doing in the home or at your hearth. If you feel you need to speak during a moment you define as spiritual or magical working, speak from the heart, or use a short prayer or poem that you already know and can apply to several situations. (See Chapter 10 for suggestions about spoken magic and prayers.)

In essence, magic is the art of clearly focusing your will to help create a change or transition of some kind. If you're familiar with the contemporary practice of magic, particularly in conjunction with your spiritual practice, then you know that certain symbols or objects can help you focus and lend energy to help accomplish that change. If you're interested in this kind of work as a supplement to your spiritual practice, I suggest that you read a book specifically focusing on magic and spellwork, such as *Power Spellcraft for Life*. As this book focuses mainly on maintaining a home-based spiritual practice instead of taking a shallower but broader survey of the practices involved in the hedge witch's path, there isn't a lot of magic-based work here. It does include folk wisdom and home-based tradition, however, which some people may identify or define as magic.

How does this all tie in to spirituality? Every moment is an opportunity to be in the now, to appreciate the moment and to make it magical. By doing this, you acknowledge that even the simplest of tasks informs your spirit and can nurture your soul. Allowing yourself to be in the moment illustrates how special you are. Life is made of many tiny moments strung together, after all. Opening yourself to the simplest of tasks and allowing it to inspire you with some insight or wisdom, or even a moment of peace, illustrates that the Divine can whisper to you in the oddest of unexpected places. Hearthcraft is about communing with the Divine through everyday tasks, not through complicated formal ritual. Pouring milk into your tea is about as simple as you can get.

Your Home as Your Spiritual Headquarters

In essence, hearthcraft operates on the level of the home. The hearth-based hedge witch seeks to create and maintain the best possible home atmosphere for family and friends, to support, fuel, and nourish them on both a physical and spiritual level.

There is a common understanding that a house is a neutral structure, and a home is a living, thriving place that is created by the actions and intentions of the people who live within that house. The home is a sanctuary, a place of security. It is defined by the people who live in it, created by them, and keyed to their energy. Energy defines the home in more than one way: it feeds and propels it spiritually and emotionally, but it is also invested in the form of money that sets it up and maintains it. Mortgage payments, rent, furnishings, consumables are all fueled by energy in the form of money, which is earned by an individual through work or other exchange of energy. Emotion, time, and money are all valid forms of energy that go into running a household and home.

Although many people use the terms "house" and "home" interchangeably, there is a difference between them and each term is used to describe something specific in this book. "House" refers to the physical dwelling, the four walls and the roof over your head; the civic address and geographic location of your residence. "Home" refers to the energy entity created by that physical dwelling, the family that lives in it, and the gestalt identity that arises from the interaction between the two.

The home is where we build a base or headquarters from where we may venture out into the world, and to which we may return at the end of the day. It is a place where we can be ourselves, where we can relax and allow the energy we control so tightly outside its walls to flow freely in a protected space. It makes an excellent and very immediate base for a spiritual practice.

Denise Linn, author of *Sacred Space*, says, "Homes are symbolic representations of ourselves, and in fact in a deeper sense are extensions of ourselves." She is absolutely right. On an unconscious level, how we treat our living space can very often give us insight into how we perceive ourselves. On a more active level, by consciously controlling how we organize and decorate our living space, we can impact our sense of self as well, and influence how we feel. Environment affects our emotional, physical, and mental functioning; it makes sense that it affects our spiritual well-being, too.

For many of us it's important to have a room or defined space within the home that is exclusively ours: a bedroom, a corner, an office or reading room. What is often overlooked is a communal area that is equally invested in with conscious awareness, and cared for in the way a private or personal space would be. Communal spaces in a home such as living rooms, family rooms, bathrooms, and kitchens become an aggregate of the energy of all the people who use them and the activities that take place within them.

Rather than allowing the energy to form willy-nilly without any sort of conscious direction, and living with whatever the result is, it's wise to take it in hand and guide the energy-signature identity. In the next chapter, we'll explore the idea of how this impacts the spiritual health and well-being of the members of the family as well.

Energy is fluid and always moving, so the result is never permanent. Ongoing maintenance is ideal. And it's never too late to begin, or to work to reverse the energy signature of a communal room that is unwelcoming or uncomfortable in some way.

To maintain, guide, and shape the energy of a communal room is a form of caring for the health and well-being of the people who use it.

The Role of Family and Community

The practice of hearthcraft presupposes someone to care for, even if it is only yourself, or your pets. Family is one of the cornerstones of hearthcraft.

Members of the family (and/or the residents of the home) are active participants in shaping and affecting the energy of the home. They maintain and continually nourish the spiritual element of the home by being active, communicative, loving, and physically present. They provide energy for the hearth-based hedge witch to function, and one of the reasons for the practice. The living energy is important to the path. Without it, the home becomes more of a house. The active, fluid, ever-changing dynamic of family and community ensures input and activity, essential elements of the spiritual well-being of the home. It is also important to remember that the family's interaction and support goes beyond maintaining the general identity of the home, however: the family supports itself as individuals as well.

Increasingly, people are no longer members of a defined religious group, and thus it falls to the family to engage in spiritual support. This can be challenging, especially when you think about all the morals, ethics, and values that an organized religion defines and instills in its adherents. These three terms are slippery and sometimes are confused.

+ **Morals:** standards of behavior, or principles of right and wrong.
+ **Ethics:** the moral principles governing or influencing conduct.
+ **Values:** principles or standards of behavior. **Value** (singular): the regard that something is held to deserve; importance or worth.

Because these three definitions are so closely intertwined, let's simplify them:

- Morals are the principles of right and wrong.
- Ethics are the application of morals to one's behavior.
- Values are morals and ethics that an individual, or society as a whole, considers important and worthy of upholding.

Define what morals are important to you, and actively demonstrate them through ethical behavior, especially at the hearth. As the hearth is considered the source point for spiritual nurturing in the home, those who live in that home and interact with the hearth should hold a very clear idea of what the paramount morals, ethics, and values of the family are in order to respect the hearth as much as possible.

The Oxford Dictionary defines "family values" as values supposedly characteristic of a traditional family unit, typically those of high moral standards and discipline. It provokes deep thought as to what moral standards and discipline are required to live an ethical life, and where that discipline comes from.

If your family is open to discussing spirituality, ask them for their input as well as you define the fundamental values you wish to associate with your hearth. It is only fair to include them and their beliefs, as what goes on at the hearth and in the home impacts and affects them as well. It can be quite illuminating to learn what morals and ethics your partner or children value, and they may surprise you by listing principles that you hadn't initially thought of.

Here's an exercise you can engage in with your family, or alone if you live by yourself. With your family, have a brainstorming session where you talk about morals, ethics, and values. Once the session is over, schedule another meeting a couple of days later. Discuss the overall list that was created during the brainstorming session. From the global list, write down the ones that mean the most to the family. Put it on the fridge or pin it to a bulletin board so everyone can see it on a regular basis. For each item on the list, come up with a real-life example. For example, if one of the values is "eco-awareness," an example might be "taking lunch to work in a reusable lunch bag or bento box." An illustration for "compassion" might be "making someone a cup of tea and sitting down with them to show that someone cares about them."

Looking up each word on the list in the dictionary and reading out the definition may be illuminating as well, because the popular idea of the meaning of things like "compassion" and "generosity" may not be what the term actually means. The family might discuss the difference between the dictionary definition and their understanding of the term, and choose one meaning over the other if it bears more ethical weight with them and has a more positive influence on the way they wish to live their lives.

One of the essential elements of the hearthcraft path is a presupposition of a community of some kind to care for, whether it be yourself and a pet, your family, or your circle of friends. Most hearth-based hedge witches gravitate to the path because they feel the need to care for and nurture those who are close to them. A kitchen and a home are places where *living people* operate and interact. These people are literally the soul of the home, much as the hearth and fireplace are the heart of the house. As a result, the hearth-based hedge witch and her work can have a significant impact on her family and extended community as they interact within her sphere. The energy you maintain in your home will affect them, just as the energy they bring to your spiritual hearth will help to fuel it.

Hearthcraft posits a certain connection to community. The term "community" can sometimes be misleading, because we often associate it with a collection of people at large from a general area. The term can comprise any collection of people who are associated in pursuit of a similar goal.

Blood isn't the only indicator of close ties. The term "kin" is sometimes employed to describe those who are members of our blood family unit, but the term "akin" means something or someone essentially similar. People who have interests or philosophies akin to yours, with whom you have a spark of connection, and whom you invite into your home constitute a community of sorts as well. We all have close friends who hold special places in our hearts, like-minded individuals who support and love us. In essence, they are family without the blood or legal ties.

"Chosen family" is the term my loved ones and I use to describe this circle. Chosen family is one such example of a close circle or community for whom our hearthcraft practices resonate in some way, whether they consciously know of your spiritual focus or not. Caring for them in emotional and physical ways—the supportive phone call, the cup of tea, the casserole in times of stress—is another way in which hearthcraft expresses itself. Caring for family and community to foster an environment that supports healthy growth and development at all levels is one of the things a hearth-based hedge witch does.

Nurturing and Nourishing

The path of the hearth-based hedge witch is rooted in the parallel paths of nurturing and nourishing. What do these words mean? The *Oxford Dictionary* defines "to nurture" as "[to] rear and encourage the development of (a child); [to] cherish (a hope, belief, or ambition)." The noun is defined as "the action or process of nurturing; upbringing, education, and environment as a factor determining personality" (emphasis mine). It defines "to nourish" as to "provide with the food or other substances necessary for growth and health; [to] keep (a feeling or belief) in one's mind for a long time." (Again, emphasis mine.)

These two definitions describe a lot of hearthcraft in a nutshell: providing both physical and environmental sustenance in order to support growth, health, and development. Hearthcraft seeks to nourish and nurture on a spiritual level as well as the physical level. Let's explore why the basics of caring for someone are so important.

Food and Shelter:
Two Basic, and Yet Not-So-Basic, Needs

Food and shelter are two of the most basic things an individual requires in order to live a good life. The concept of hearth and home reflects both of these things: warmth, protection, and food. These may seem to be comparatively insignificant when compared to other more lofty things to be aiming for in life, but in reality, these basic needs have to be fulfilled in order to enable us to explore the higher potential of our lives and spirits.

Abraham Maslow's Hierarchy of Needs demonstrates this requirement. Maslow's Hierarchy of Needs posits a chain of needs, each rooted in the previous one. The Hierarchy of Needs demonstrates that fundamental physical requirements such as food, shelter, and protection are valid needs that must be addressed in order to create the security and liberate the energy required to pursue other needs that are classified higher in the hierarchy Maslow outlined, such as creating an aesthetically pleasing environment or pursuing understanding of the self within the community. Maslow's theory isn't absolute, but it does provide a useful explanation for humanity's focus on the concept of hearth and home, and why it seems to be so ingrained in our cultures and psyches.

Maslow's hierarchy is as follows:

1. Basic physical needs, such as food and shelter.
2. Safety needs, such as protection from the elements and a feeling of security from the unknown.
3. The need for love and belonging, within a small social unit and a larger community.
4. Self-esteem needs, or confirming the sense of acceptance within the community, from which issues the sense of self-worth.
5. The need for understanding, again from the community within which one operates.

6. Aesthetic needs, or being able to manipulate one's environment in a desired way to reflect beauty or another value.
7. The need for self-actualization, which can be interpreted as self-improvement, feeling rewarded or satisfied by your life, as well as the impetus to strive for more.
8. Transcendence and peak experience, the culmination of the process of self-actualization and the ultimate spiritual escape from the material world: the absence of need.

Hearthcraft tends to focus on securing and maintaining the earlier needs. This is far from being simplistic or primitive: every single person requires at least the first two needs of food and protection in order to survive. Hearthcraft is rooted in these primary needs, making it a necessary and highly respected path. Without the assurance of these basic needs, you cannot go on to explore more exalted paths, or seek more challenging paths in life. In the end, the focal issues addressed in hearthcraft are required by every single person in some way, shape, or form.

Knowing this, it is still hard to believe that there are people who dismiss the idea that anyone who works to maintain a secure and happy home is missing something or limiting themselves in some way. The casual dismissal of men or women who have chosen to follow a domestic-centered path as second-class citizens, for example, is shameful when one looks at cultural mores and stories where a woman was queen within her house, who managed and ordered and made sure the family had a safe, warm, secure, and successful base from which to operate, thereby maximizing their chances of success in their chosen paths. With basic needs met and accounted for, you can focus your energy on the higher, more spiritual needs, such as self-actualization and transcendence. Practicing hearthcraft is an excellent method whereby confidence and self-esteem may be secured through answering basic needs. The more control you have over the energy and function of your home environment, the more likely you and your family are to be relaxed and happy. When you are relaxed, there are fewer obstacles to divert the life-renewing energy flowing through your life. Stress, anxiety, and fear commonly snarl up and divert the energy flowing through our lives. Keeping a welcoming, serene, and happy hearth maximizes your potential to create a successful life, resting upon the firm foundation built at the hearth, in the spiritual heart of the home.

Kitchen Witchcraft

There are many other traditions that possess an element of hearthcraft to them, but the most familiar of them is likely to be kitchen witchcraft. As I explained above, I differentiate the two paths by emphasizing the spiritual element found in the path of the hearth-based hedge witch, as opposed to the more magic-based path of the kitchen witch.

A kitchen witch is someone who practices magic through cooking, baking, and other kitchen-based activity. Patricia Telesco, arguably kitchen witchery's most visible practitioner, says in her book *A Kitchen Witch's Cookbook*, "Since we all have to prepare food at one time or another, why not make the best possible use of that time in the kitchen?"

The kitchen witch is a figure also familiar for her use as a kitchen icon or good luck charm. Regardless of the spiritual path followed by the family, many homes feature a small witch doll, usually astride a broom, hanging somewhere in the kitchen. This little talisman is said to bring successful cooking and good luck to the residents of and visitors to the kitchen. Perhaps more precisely, they are said to guard against failed cooking or cooking disasters. German folklore has it that they guard specifically against dough failing to rise, milk curdling, and fallen cakes. The dolls are made of many different materials. Some are corn husk dolls; some have dried apples for heads; others are made entirely of fabric. The earliest appearance of these kitchen icons are in German and Scandinavian traditions.

There are other parallels to the kitchen witch doll. As a harvest custom, communities in Britain and Europe would tie together the last sheaf of wheat, and keep it over the winter as good luck and protection. Sometimes the sheaf was draped with cloth or otherwise dressed and adorned. Other communities would weave the first or last stalks cut in the harvest into various shapes of different sizes, including geometric shapes and animal forms. Confusingly, these were also called corn dollies, even when they were not in human form. The term "dolly" is thought to be derived from the word "idol." These customs stemmed from the belief that the first or last stalks of wheat that were cut contained the spirit of the crop. By keeping it in a place of honor and safety over the winter, the farmers would in essence be protecting the success of next year's crops. The dolly was often ploughed into the fields when the time came to prepare them for the spring planting, or burned after the harvest as an offering to the harvest deities. Sometimes the sheaf is referred to as the harvest queen, the corn mother, or corn maiden, and there are a wide variety of shapes into which the stalks are woven, according to local tradition. The art is still practiced today, and is called both corn dolly plaiting and wheat weaving. Beautiful abstract shapes and designs are created, as well as figures and religious objects.

If you wish to make your own protective kitchen witch icon, a craft detailing how to make a corn husk doll that can be used may be found in Chapter 10. Making a new one every year is certainly a possibility, after disposing of the old one by burning or shredding it and mixing it into your compost or mulch. It's a nice tradition to link to Thanksgiving, the autumnal equinox, or any of the harvest festivals found in various religious calendars. It may also be tied into a purification ritual, with the dismantling of the old, symbolizing the clearing of accumulated negativity or stale energy, and the introduction of the new, symbolizing a fresh start.

Chapter Two

Hearth and Home as Sacred Space

The central concept of hearth and home-based spirituality puts forth that the home is sacred. But what does sacred really mean? *Sacer,* the Latin root of the term, means "holy." The *Oxford Dictionary* defines "sacred" as "connected with a deity and so deserving veneration; holy." Alternatively, it may mean "religious rather than secular." In plainer terms, this means that if something is considered sacred it is recognized as being touched by the realm of the gods in some way, and therefore something that we consider worthy of respect or honor. If so touched, it is theoretically no longer of this world: it is set apart, and revered or honored for this reason. Note that "set apart" does not mean isolated and worshipped. Instead, it means given honor within the context of the everyday world.

Sacred space, then, is a zone where we can touch the Divine, communicate with it, interact with it, or be influenced by it in a way that is clearer (or more easily perceived or felt) than in other places. We generally recognize certain sites as sacred. Sites of grave tragedy, such as Auschwitz; sites of great beauty; sites consecrated to a particular religion, such as Chartres Cathedral or the Taj Mahal; sites historically significant, such as where peace treaties were signed, battles fought, and great people met; sites of commemoration, such as cemeteries and burial grounds; and sites of ancient activity, the purpose of which are now lost to us, such as Stonehenge. Part of the mystery of sacred space is how it is simultaneously familiar to us, and yet we can sense that there is something "other" about it. This tension is part of what we recognize when we sense that a place or object is sacred.

To consecrate something means to ritually designate it as sacred. While this action is found in many alternative spiritual paths as well as formal religions, it doesn't figure largely in hearthcraft. This is mainly due to the recognition that there is a touch of the sacred in all things, and the hearth is especially sacred due to its function. There is no call to formally consecrate the hearth, because it is already sacred.

It is important to remember that in hearthcraft the areas, actions, and times you hold sacred are not isolated from the everyday world; they are very much a part of it, and lend their sanctity to what and who interacts with them. In other words, *we are blessed by interacting with what we consider sacred.* This is one of the most important precepts of hearth and home-based spirituality: by caring for and maintaining your home, you simultaneously enhance its sanctity while it touches and blesses you.

The Home as Sacred Space

We guard our homes; we defend them from unwanted intruders, both physical and otherwise. We invest great amounts of money in them, whether we rent or own them. We decorate them in a way that soothes us, or enlivens us, or reflects us in some way.

Inviting someone into our home is a great concession. It says "I trust you" in some way. We trust a guest to behave well, to be considerate, and to appreciate the personal space that is ours.

The Japanese culture demonstrates how highly it respects the sanctity of the home by having people remove their shoes before entering a dwelling. It shows respect for the hosts by abstaining from ruining the floor covering (originally *tatami*, a woven plant fiber like straw that is easily damaged by footwear), as well as avoiding tracking dirt into the home. Symbolically, removing the footwear also represents leaving the worries and problems experienced outside at the door.

To define the space between the outside world and the private space of the home, there is an entryway referred to as the *genkan*, where the footwear is removed and stored in a cupboard or shelf divided into a series of cubes called a *getabako*. The genkan functions as a buffer between the sacred space of the private home and the uncontrolled outside world. The level of the actual living space is usually one step up from the entryway, and this step functions as another kind of buffer, requiring you to physically step up and away from both the outside world and the transitional area. There is an entire etiquette associated with the genkan and how shoes are removed and placed, and how to enter the home as well. Japan isn't the only culture to employ this custom. Parts of Korea, China, Indochina, and down through Southeast Asia also have customs involving the removal of footwear before entering sacred places.

In Japan, footwear is removed before entering shrines and temples, and some restaurants. Many homes also provide slippers for visitors to wear once they have removed their outdoor footwear. A different pair of slippers are worn in the bathroom and are not to be worn outside it, further demonstrating how the different energies of the home are kept as separate as possible.

The custom of removing one's hat before entering a home is also associated with respect. In Western culture, hats are removed to demonstrate respect for a person, a place, an action, or to illustrate recognition of one's humbler station. Hats are removed by men in a Christian church to humble oneself before God; however, some sects require that women cover their heads before entering the church. Hats are generally worn outdoors, and to wear one inside smacks of poor breeding as well as disrespect for the sanctity of the place. Conversely, however, Judaism instructs their adherents to always cover their heads in a temple, usually with a yarmulke or kippah.

The home is set apart as sacred space, apart from and separate from the outside world. Within the home there are further zones of sacred space, the hearth being the zone of focus in this book. Sacred spaces are recognized by our deference to them and defense of them: they are sacred to us. Some spaces are recognizable by other people as sacred: the collection of family portraits on a shelf, for example, or a collection of statuary. Sacred things have a certain aura to them, and we are both drawn to them and understand innately that we ought not to touch or interfere with them. This aura can originate from the item itself, which may have drawn you to acquire it in the first place, or be instilled in it by your designation of it as sacred. The former may have come about by the item's previous associations, or its origins.

There are sacred spaces that are almost universally recognized, and sacred spaces that are unique to one or a small group of individuals. Something can very well be sacred to you and no one else, and that's fine. A space or object does not have to be validated as sacred by anyone else for it to have power for you. While you may not sense the sanctity of a place or item held sacred by someone else, it is always courteous to respect the other person's sense of sanctity.

In most Neo-Pagan traditions as well as formal religious organizations, sacred space is created by intent. It is important to stress that in hearth-craft, sacred space is not created but recognized. No actions are necessary on the part of the practitioner. The hearth is considered sacred as a matter of custom. You may wish to honor it, or perform ceremonies to maintain its purity, but in essence, the home is a sacred place to begin with, and thus needs little more than ceremonial recognition.

The Hearth as Sacred Space

The hearth symbolizes sacred space wherein you can be yourself, where you are secure, where you can be open. It is a wellspring of sorts. It is a place where you can access energy, wisdom, and power more easily than anywhere else within your home, and outside it for that matter. It is a place where you can explore your thoughts and feelings, a place of communion with family and the Divine, a place where you can stand to direct that energy, wisdom, and power to a greater good on a family level and the level of your community. The hearth is a place of power.

It is this purpose that the hearth serves within the home. The hearth is a wellspring, a place where people can recharge, where they can go for comfort on a basic level.

When we use the term "hearth," it generally evokes a vague idea of the symbol for the essence of home, in the form of a fireplace of some kind. People who possess a fireplace or know a bit about history may be able to identify it specifically as part of the fireplace layout. Since the word is central to this book, let's take a moment to explore the various definitions of what a hearth is.

Here's an interesting fact for you. The term "focus" (plural: foci) is a Latin word meaning hearth, fireplace; fire, flame; center; or central point. How appropriate, then, that the hearth is considered the focus of home-based spirituality.

"Hearth" is defined variously as the brick or stone-lined space at the base of a chimney where a fire can be built and at which cooking takes place; the stone- or brick-paved, tiled, or otherwise protected area next to or surrounding a fireplace, that extends out into the room; the likewise paved flat surface on which a stove sits (especially an iron wood-burning stove); and the figurative home built around the fireplace as symbolic center.

It is this last definition that most people think of first.

As an extension of the fireplace, the hearth is a natural place to gather. In older times, the fireside was a place where chores were done—sometimes out of necessity if the fire was an essential part of the task—sometimes for light, warmth, or comfort. It is a social place as well as a place to work. Soap-making, candle-making, and dyeing all require heat and water when done by hand, for example. Caring for the young, the elderly, or the ill would also have been done near the fire, for its light and warmth. The hearth was centrally located in most simple homes, making it a natural gathering place for social reasons as well as practical ones. Lessons and teaching would also take place by the hearth.

In short, the hearth is a very active zone of the kitchen area, and of the home overall.

Sacred Fire

The home is recognized as being sacred, set apart from the outside world. As seen above, within this set-apart zone there is a further sacred zone: the hearth, the location of the central fire of a home. In essence, the fireplace functioning as a symbolic center of a home exemplifies the concept of the hearth as a sacred fire.

Fire is seen as sacred in many, many cultures. Remember, the definition of "sacred" is something recognized as being touched by the realm of the gods in some way, and therefore something that we consider worthy of respect or honor. Therefore, the hearthfire as something sacred means a place where the spiritual world intersects with the profane or everyday world: it is a place or object through which communication can take place.

Why is fire considered sacred? Fire is also a symbol of vitality, for it "lives," "eats," and "breathes." When it burns, it symbolizes the spark of life that animates us. Fire is one of the four physical elements the ancients recognized as the building-blocks of the world. It is the element that is recognized as being alive more than the other three, due to its nature: it appears to have a mind of its own, it eats, it sleeps, it dies. Mankind must respect both its useful properties and its destructive properties as well: fire destroys indiscriminately, with rage and a primal fury that mankind can only attempt to control, but that destruction very often purifies in preparation for regrowth and new creations.

Fire has played an important role in several religions. The symbol of the eternal flame is a common concept in several religions; it has also been used to symbolize the presence of the Divine. In Christian myth, for example, God manifested as a burning bush; the sanctity of the flame was demonstrated by how it did not consume the bush itself as fuel.

Fire has been a method by which offerings are made, and a method of divination.

Examples of fire-based festivals from various cultures include Diwali, the Hindu festival of lights, and Hanukkah, the Jewish festival commemorating the miracle of a one-day supply of lamp oil burning for eight days in the newly reconsecrated temple of Jerusalem.

Fire is a symbol of spiritual energy, as is the sun, and indeed shares many traits and energies with the solar luminary. As a spiritual symbol, fire illuminates personal/emotional/spiritual darkness, which may be why so many religions use candles and oil-based flames as part of their temple and church tools and accouterments. Modern earth-based religions and occult-based paths are no different: candles are frequently used to symbolize energy of all kinds, activity, illumination, and faith, among other things.

The Hearth Fire at Home: A Heart Both Spiritual and Practical

In times past, the fire played an important role in the home. It was a source of light and warmth, and it cooked food. These basic needs were impossible to achieve without a fire. Starting a fire was a time-consuming task, and so the hearth fire was banked at night to keep the coals and embers alive in order to use it as a basis for the next day's fire. The kitchen fire was crucial to daily life; to allow it to go out demonstrated unpreparedness. It was a sacred task of sorts to conscientiously think ahead, to maintain a basic supply of fuel, to keep the house in order and running smoothly. The absence of a fire, whether through negligence or otherwise, meant the lack of warmth, a method by which nourishing food could be prepared, protection, and so forth. The parable of the wise and foolish virgins from the Old Testament demonstrates the importance of being prepared for household tasks such as tending the fire.

In Ireland, the only time the household fire was intentionally allowed to go out was at Beltaine, the festival that modern spiritual paths place at the beginning of May. A main fire was lit at Tara, the spiritual center of Ireland, by the king or the druids, and from this fire all the other household fires were symbolically relit. This practice demonstrated unity throughout the kingdom as well as recognizing the spiritual power of the monarch or the druids.

Fuel for the fire is as important as the fire itself. Oil in particular serves as the fuel for many spiritually symbolic flames. Oil was (and is now again becoming) a precious commodity. Generally extracted from plant matter, it was so valuable that it was used as an offering to deities, and as gifts to churches and temples. You can do the same by offering a thimbleful of oil to your hearth spirits on a regular basis at a schedule of your choosing. For ideas on incorporating an oil lamp into your spiritual practice, see later on in this chapter.

Bonfires and Needfires

The sacred fire also manifested in the form of bonfires, sometimes called needfires.

The needfire was a custom by which a bonfire was kindled for a specific spiritual purpose. The exact purpose depends on which culture is kindling the fire. Some of these fires were required to be lit by the friction method (rubbing two sticks together, or some variation thereon); others required a certain number of people to build them, or a certain combination of woods, or to be lit at a certain time of day. Often, the bonfire had to be the only fire burning within a certain distance; if another flame burned within its specified boundary the power of the needfire would be rendered ineffective. Sometimes, this bonfire would serve as the source from which all the previously extinguished home fires were relit, or to produce smoke through which cattle or other livestock would be driven in order to protect them from illness. The practice of building and lighting a needfire or bonfire underlines the folk belief in the ability of fire to purify or bless, an extension of its innate sanctity.

Making a Cauldron-Based Needfire

Not everyone has the acreage or the fuel (or can obtain a permit) to build an outdoor bonfire. As most modern homes don't have a fireplace, and many towns have bylaws about building a fire in your backyard (if you have one), this is an excellent way to create a small, time-defined sacred fire.

Make sure your cauldron will be strong enough to withstand intense heat. If your cauldron, or the vessel you use as a cauldron, is not made of cast iron or a material designed to withstand intense heat, do not use it for this task. The heat will cause materials such as ceramics or glass to shatter. If you have a fireplace, you can put your cauldron on the hearth while you burn the needfire. Otherwise, place the heatproof trivet, pad, or stone under the cauldron and make sure the cauldron sits securely on it. Never put the cauldron on a wooden or fabric-covered surface.

While rubbing alcohol is specified in the list of supplies below because it is inexpensive and easily found, you can use any high-percentage alcohol available in liquor stores, such as ethanol (grain alcohol, such as Everclear) or liquors like vodka or brandy. These make lovely offerings to a deity or spirit. Remember, the higher the percentage of alcohol in the liquor the hotter the fire, and plan accordingly. Make sure your room is ventilated; while this fire does not produce toxic gases or smoke, it does get very, very hot.

For a cauldron fire, you will need:

+ Epsom salts
+ Rubbing alcohol
+ Blend of herbs and resins (your choice)

- Measuring cup
- Long-handled match
- Heatproof trivet or pad, or a flat stone
- Large bowl of sand
- Lid for the cauldron (make sure it is heavy)
- Fire extinguisher (CO_2 or dry chemical)

1. Measure out equal parts of Epsom salts and alcohol. Place the salts in the bottom of the cauldron, and pour the alcohol over them.
2. Pour the herbal mixture into the cauldron. Place the cauldron on the trivet or heatproof stone.
3. Light the long-handled match and touch it to the mixture. It will burst into almost silent flame, the tops of the flames leaping above the cauldron. The fire will burn until the alcohol has been consumed. Throughout the fire, but more so when the flames begin to die away, you will hear tiny pops and sizzles as the salt cracks in the heat and the herbs and resins are consumed by the flames.

Do not even think about adding more alcohol into the cauldron while the flames are burning! Keep the alcohol/salt proportion as equal until you are confident about handling the resulting fire; then and only then may you tweak the proportions. Never simply pour a large amount of alcohol over the salts; the resulting flames can be several feet high and cause major damage to you or your house. Be safe, and use common sense.

I cannot stress how dangerous this activity can be if you do not approach it with respect and common sense. There is a reason why the last three items in the supply list are there: the heavy lid is to smother the flames if they get out of hand, and the bag of sand or earth is to pour over it all if you need to douse it immediately. The suggested fire extinguisher is there as further backup.

Do not leap over this fire, or ever leave it unattended. As with all other flame-based objects or exercises watch your sleeves and hair, and make sure you set the cauldron away from anything flammable such as curtains.

Instead of adding herbs directly to the salt, you can steep your selected herbs or flowers in the alcohol you plan to use. Steep them for at least two weeks, then strain and bottle the alcohol. Label it clearly and do not use it for any other purpose.

The Epsom salts soak up some of the alcohol and keep the fire burning in a more stable fashion. The flames will consume the herbs and resins you added, so this is also a lovely way to make an offering or to cleanse a room. This is a wonderful way to scry, or meditate by watching the flames. The fire dies away within a handful of minutes, depending on how much alcohol there is in the cauldron.

The Practice of Smooring

Smooring is a term encountered often in Celtic prayer, and it means banking a fire. In this modern age even the phrase "banking a fire" may be mysterious. From the context in which it's generally found one can infer that it is something done to preserve a fire in some way so that it may be revived the next morning. And it's almost that simple. To bank a fire literally means to build up a protective wall of ashes or stones around the coals in order to keep it from spreading dangerously while you sleep, and to protect it from drafts and disturbances. By protecting the coals in this way, they can be used as the basis for building a new fire the next day. If the fire is outdoors and you intend to use it for more than one day, you can plan to build it next to a rock or dirt wall to help shelter it in this way. A fire ring or pit at a campground is basically this sort of design.

The word "bank" when used as a verb means to "heap or form into a mass or mound," and that's precisely what's done to bank a fire. You don't cover the coals or embers entirely; that would smother them and have the opposite effect of what you're intending. Scrape the coals and embers together, then scrape the ashes up around them, insulating them. If you need more insulation, use rocks. If you're banking in a fireplace, close the flue and the fire doors, if you have them.

Since most people have electricity to provide light and heat, smooring is a skill and a practice that has generally fallen out of disuse. In a spiritual context, however, it provides an opportunity to gather yourself back into yourself, in a manner of speaking, to pull your energy back from all the different directions in which the day has scattered it. In essence, it's a moment of personal reconnection with the self. You can think of it as banking your personal flame, if you like, caring for it in such a way that it is sheltered and protected overnight, and ready for use the next day.

Do this after you have finished cleaning up and tidying, and just before you head to bed. You can try doing it before and after you prepare yourself for bed; one way may be more useful for you and provide a better effect. The goal is to evaluate the day without judgment. You can do this in the kitchen, or anywhere else in your home. If the weather is good you may wish to do it outside, on the back porch or steps.

1. Stand or sit with a relaxed frame. If you know a relaxation exercise, run through it to rid yourself of any excess stress and tension in your body.

2. Think back to how you felt when you woke up, and then think back over your day's activities. Take note of how they made you feel, be it happy, angry, frustrated, sad, or peaceful; remember, this retrospective isn't done with the intent to judge how you handled yourself, simply to accept the day as it was, and yourself as you are. This doesn't have to be a long step; you don't have to think through every event in detail. Call them up as impressions.

3. When you have finished thinking back over the day, close your eyes and take three slow, deep breaths. As you exhale each breath, allow any fear or worry or irritation connected with the day flow out of you.

4. Feel yourself here, now, at this moment, and accept yourself. If you like, at this point you may say a brief prayer, or a simple

phrase such as, "I accept myself. Watch over me as I sleep, spirits of the hearth, and guard my loved ones and our home. I bid you good night."

5. As the final act, do something physical and symbolic of finishing the day. You could turn off the light (be it the kitchen light or wherever you are), or close the door if you have been outside or standing at the door. If you have been sitting with a candle, using the flame as a meditative and calming focus, snuff it out either by blowing it out, pinching it, or using a candle snuffer.

If you like, you can say a prayer in place of the phrase included above. You may already have a prayer that fits the purpose, or you may wish to write a new one. Saying a prayer that offers you an opportunity to connect with the Divine or the spirits of your hearth affirms your connection to it or them.

This is the traditional smooring prayer used in the Highlands of Scotland, as collected by Alexander Carmichael in the *Carmina Gadelica*. It calls on both Mary and Brigid (invoked here as Bride, a Scottish version of the name) as deities of domestic life to bless the home and the inhabitants. If you like, you can substitute other deity names, or simply use the term "the Divine" to encompass your concept of God. The original prayer reads as follows:

I will smoor the hearth
As Mary would smoor;
The encompassment of Bride and of Mary,

On the fire and on the floor,
And on the household all.
Who is on the lawn without?
Fairest Mary and her Son,
The mouth of God ordained, the angel of God spoke;
Angels of promise watching the hearth,
Till white day comes to the fire.

Chapter Three

Working with the Spiritual Hearth

Hearthcraft posits recognizing that your home is a sacred place, and a place that has the power to refresh you, relax you, and rejuvenate you. Apart from the general effect it will have upon you as you function within it, how precisely can you intentionally tap into this power? This chapter explores methods in which you can work with the spiritual hearth.

The spiritual hearth represents a refuge from the outside world, as well as a sacred place designed and maintained to maximize spiritual benefit. Deliberately designing a place of beauty, a place of serenity and calm, can be a challenge. First of all, you'll have to deal with the physical limitations or drawbacks of the physical building in which you're living. It's rare that we can live in the ideal home of our dreams. You'll also have to deal with the needs and preferences of the other people who live in your house, and your budget. Making the most of what you have is part of the practical aspect of hearthcraft. This is one of the main reasons why the spiritual hearth revolves around the energy and atmosphere of the home, both of which can be cultivated by behavior, attitude, and positive outlook, instead of physical or tangible rearranging or redecorating. Although the latter can certainly enhance your home and the effect you are seeking to achieve, it's important to remember that the spiritual hearth functions on the level of energy and spiritual benefit.

Locating the Spiritual Hearth: The Heart of Your Home

The spiritual hearth is the symbolic heart of your home. Although the kitchen seems to be the logical modern parallel of the physical hearth, it doesn't necessarily have to be the spiritual hearth of your home. Many people have to live with kitchens that are poorly laid out, seemingly afterthoughts of the architect. A kitchen that is cramped or unwelcoming is very definitely not the symbolic heart of your home. If this is the case with you, think about how the areas of your home are used and where people seem to gravitate, to help you determine where the symbolic heart of your home is. Perhaps everyone brings their various activities into the living room, or dining room, or family room. Perhaps the curve of a staircase where there is a window overlooking the garden is where people unconsciously pause. Or perhaps the spiritual center of your home is where you can feel the rest of it around you, even if the physical center is in a hallway or an odd spot.

If you can't put your finger on the heart of your home, and you do not wish to designate your kitchen as the symbolic hearth, then consciously choose another area. If you have a fireplace, this makes an excellent physical representation of the spiritual hearth, provided that it is in a room that sees frequent use. There is no point to establishing a symbolic hearth in an unused fireplace located in a room that people avoid.

Creating a Physical Representation of the Spiritual Hearth

Once you have determined or chosen the heart of your home and designated it as the physical location to represent the spiritual hearth, you can perform a purification and blessing (see Chapter 7) or the ritual to recognize the sanctity of the hearth, which may be found at the end of this chapter. This physical representation of the spiritual hearth can be used as a location to focus your spiritual activity. You may wish to create an altar or a shrine there, or use it as a place to meditate, or pray, and as a place to stand when you wish to draw strength or energy from the spiritual hearth. You may choose to designate it in a different way, such as hanging a particular piece of artwork there, or by positioning a small wall shelf with an oil lamp on it, or any other method you feel appropriate to you and your home. You may simply use it as the place from where you begin your cleaning or tidying activity. For more information on altars and shrines see Chapter 6.

Chapter 6 also explores the kitchen as a logical location for the spiritual work and is worth reading even if you feel that the spiritual center of your home is located elsewhere, as much of our daily activity is kitchen associated and provides opportunity for spiritual activity.

Ritual for Recognizing the Sanctity of the Hearth

As this chapter has stated above, there is no need to consecrate the hearth because it is innately sacred. However, many people like to perform some kind of ritual formally recognizing an existing sanctity, and so this ritual has been included. It can be used on a regular basis as you wish, or performed when you feel your focal hearth area has become cluttered with other energies that may not be negative but may occlude your personal connection to the hearth. As the hearth is your source of power and energy, keeping the connection to it clear also means that the energy flowing from it moves more freely.

The items you will need are representations of the four elements, drawn from your kitchen. You don't need a lot of each item; a teaspoon would be enough. You may place them in bowls before you on the floor, or on a table by you. They should be within arm's reach so that you do not need to move. The candle may be any candle at all—an emergency candle, a tea light, a birthday candle stuck into a small ball of clay, dough, or even a crumpled up bit of tinfoil or chunk of bread. Choose a color that resonates with the concept of hearth and home to you. The mixed herbs and spices should be drawn from your spice rack, a pinch of at least two different ones and as many as you like.

Although the directions indicate standing, you may kneel before the hearth if you are more comfortable doing the ritual that way.

You will need:

+ Small bowl of salt
+ Small bowl of water
+ Small bowl of mixed herbs and spices from your kitchen (see above)
+ Small bowl of olive or vegetable oil
+ Candle in candleholder (color your choice)
+ Matches

1. Stand before your hearth, wherever it may be in your home. Remember, the hearth does not need to be a physical fireplace or cooking station. Close your eyes and take three deep cleansing breaths, inhaling and exhaling slowly, with the intent of calming your body and mind. Be in the moment.
2. Open your eyes and hold your hands out to the hearth. Say:

Heart of my home,
I recognize you.
My spirit feels your warmth.
My soul feels your wisdom.
Sacred hearth, I recognize you.

3. Bow to the hearth.

4. Press your fingers into the bowl of salt, then stand up and say,

Sacred hearth,
The earth of my home recognizes your sanctity.

Flick your fingers so that the grains of salt clinging to them scatter toward and over the hearth area.

5. Dip your fingers into the water, then say,

Sacred hearth,
The water of my home recognizes your sanctity.

Flick your fingers so that the droplets of water on them scatter over the hearth area.

6. Dip your fingers in the bowl of spices and stir them so that the scent is released, then say,

Sacred hearth,
The air of my home recognizes your sanctity.

Waft your hand over the bowl, moving the scented air toward the hearth.

7. Strike a match and light the candle. Extinguish the match, laying it in a heatproof dish. Pick up the candle and hold it toward the hearth, saying,

Sacred hearth,
The fire of my home recognizes your sanctity.

Place the candle on the hearth itself, saying,

Sacred hearth,
I honor the sacred fire that burns within you.
I thank you for the wisdom, knowledge, and power
That you bring to this home.
May your sacred flame burn forever,
And may my home be ever blessed by it.

8. Dip a finger in the oil, saying,

   Sacred hearth,
   With this oil I mark you
   As a symbol of our recognition of your sanctity
   And our gratitude for your many gifts and blessings.

   Touch your oil-damp fingertip to the hearth. As your hearth may indeed be a symbolic space, make sure to not smear too much oil; a light touch will suffice.

9. Bow to the hearth one last time. Leave the candle burning if you will be working in the room, otherwise snuff it out.

The Virtual Spiritual Hearth

One of the things you can do to further develop your perception of your spiritual hearth is to create one in your imagination. This imagined version in no way replaces or supercedes the location of the spiritual hearth in your home. Instead, think of it as your idealized version of the spiritual hearth, a place you can visit in your mind while meditating or allowing your mind to wander. An imagined landscape such as this offers you unlimited access to another representation of your spiritual hearth, one that you can carry with you wherever you go. It's also a place where you can carry out activities in which you can't necessarily engage in the everyday world for whatever reason (lack of space, lack of privacy, limited physical capability, and so forth). Think of it as your virtual spiritual hearth, linked both to the physical representation of your spiritual hearth, and the actual spiritual heart of your home. Your imagined spiritual hearth can be a mental reflection of the actual physical place you have set up, or an idealized spiritual hearth.

To create it, sit in the spiritual heart of your home, in front of the physical representation you have created or chosen. Light a candle or oil lamp to represent the sacred flame of light and love that burns in the heart of the spiritual hearth. Relax your body and close your eyes, breathing deeply and slowly. Visualize a flame, such as the one you have lit. Now slowly expand your visualization to see what kind of surface the flame is resting on. What is the light like? What is the room or area around the flame like? Look at the walls (if there are any), the ground, the ceiling, or the sky. These things tend to appear in this way for a reason, usually created by your subconscious mind.

You may change these things as you desire, but think about why they have appeared in your imagination in these forms.

You are free to design your virtual spiritual hearth as you wish, but keep it simple. Remember that you are creating a space in which you want to feel safe, relaxed, serene, and still connected to your home. The space you visualize may not be very different from the physical representation you have created for your spiritual hearth, and that's absolutely fine.

When you are finished, take some time to write down what your imagined spiritual hearth looked like, or draw it. Include these notes and sketches in your home journal (see Chapter 8). If you like, you can perform a version of the above ritual to recognize the sanctity of the hearth in your imagination, too. Simply visualize performing the ritual in your virtual spiritual hearth.

Accessing Your Spiritual Hearth's Energy

One of the arguments made earlier for creating and maintaining a spiritual hearth was for the power and energy that it provides for the household. It's a symbiotic relationship: the household creates energy that feeds the spiritual hearth, which in turn nourishes and lends power to the household.

Theoretically you are always connected to your spiritual hearth, but at times it can be hard to sense the connection, especially when you are tired or stressed. When you are in need of energy to replenish your own or to shore you up, you have two options. You can draw on your spiritual hearth, or you can draw on the energy of the earth. The latter is a common technique called *grounding*.

To draw on the energy of the earth, imagine your personal energy extending a tendril of awareness down through the water, through the earth under the building, to the center of the earth. Feel how rooted you are, how connected to the world and its energy.

You can also use this technique to access the energy of your spiritual hearth. Visualize a tendril of your awareness extending to your spiritual hearth, wherever you feel that may be. You might visualize the physical location within the home that you have designated your spiritual hearth, or a shrine you have constructed (see Chapter 6), or reach out for the feeling the energy of your spiritual hearth creates. Through that tendril, absorb the energy of your spiritual hearth. Withdraw the tendril back into your energy center when you are done.

If you're unfamiliar with grounding or would like a more structured technique, here's a more detailed step-by-step process for drawing on the energy of your spiritual hearth.

1. Visualize your physical representation of your spiritual hearth or your virtual hearth. Imagine yourself standing before it.

2. Visualize a flame burning on it—a candle, an oil lamp, a needfire, or some other form. This flame represents the spiritual power of your hearth, the energy you and your family have put into it as well as the energy it produces on its own.

3. Hold your hands out to it. Imagine your hands feeling the warmth of the flame. The warmth is a form of that spiritual energy.

4. Draw that warmth into your hands, and feel it flow up your arms and into your body. Let it fill up your heart and spirit. Absorb as much as you need.

5. When you feel energized, balanced, relaxed, or however you sought out the spiritual hearth to feel, move your hands away from the flame and place your palms together. This closes the energy connection you have made to the flame, and prevents you from absorbing too much of the energy.

6. Thank your spiritual hearth in your own words, and allow the visualization to fade. Open your eyes and take a few deep slow breaths. Make sure you feel yourself fully back in the moment. Stretch gently if you like.

If you prefer an alternate visualization, instead of feeling the warmth of the flame visualize yourself absorbing the light the flame casts instead, and absorb the energy that way.

You can also channel this energy into objects or spaces as necessary. Visualize one hand absorbing the energy of the spiritual hearth and extend your other hand toward the object or area you wish to fill or empower with the energy of the spiritual hearth. This goal or target may be physically located in the real word with you, located elsewhere, or may be something intangible such as a situation. In this method, you are acting as a conduit: the hearth's energy passes through you and into the target.

Cauldron and Water Energy at the Spiritual Hearth

You'll notice I tend to phrase the energy of the spiritual hearth in terms of light and heat. This is a direct result of the primary connection between the hearth and sacred fire. However, if working with fire energy is uncomfortable for you, simply replace the visualization of a flame with a cauldron of cool water imbued with healing, comfort, and serenity. For example, in the above visualization, you can imagine placing your hands in the cauldron of water to draw the coolness of the energy up, or simply cup your hands around the cool cauldron and absorb the energy that way. (The cauldron as a symbol is explored in Chapter 4.) Experiment with both the fire and cauldron visualizations, get to know how your personal energy reacts with each symbol and kind of energy, and use them in different situations.

Ancestors and the Spiritual Hearth

Family serves as one of our connections to life. They are a source of strength as well as something to protect and care for. Living or dead, they contribute to the energy of our home. Acknowledging the contribution of ancestors, be they biological or spiritual, is a way of honoring their contribution to the world in which you live, and also of maintaining continuity of tradition. Expressing your gratitude and respect for them is one way to touch that sacred space symbolized by the hearth.

We don't consciously do what our parents or grandparents did for the sake of tradition. There's a lot of emotional energy tied up with home-based activity, however, especially creating favorite family foods. Challenge someone on how they (and by extension a relative) prepares a dish considered a family specialty and you're liable to encounter aggressive defense, if not an all-out attack. We defend our methods jealously, and by extension those family members from whom we learned them. "My mother always did it this way" is something we often say in the kitchen, whether it's making gravy, rolling gnocchi, adding a pinch of a certain secret ingredient to a soup or stew, sweeping the floor after scatting a pinch of salt on it, or soaking linen napkins after use. We absorb a lot of tradition in and around the kitchen simply being exposed to how someone else performs tasks, and by replicating those techniques we are in essence maintaining a tradition of sorts.

Ancestors are always a part of the spiritual hearth's energy. Ancestors are tied into the concept of hearth and home, both as family and as guiding energies. Like the hearth itself, your ancestors are a source of inspiration, energy, and support, a place of safety and restoration for you and your current family.

Many cultures honor or worship their ancestors. "When you drink water, think of its source" is a Chinese saying that illustrates the impact and presence ancestors can have upon your life and spiritual practice. The saying suggests that through acknowledging your ancestors you are not alone, that you come from somewhere; your ancestors anchor you in the world. Essentially, you owe what you are and what you have to work with to those who came before you.

There is no hard-and-fast rule dictating how to incorporate ancestors into your spiritual practice. Simply remembering them ties their energy into your home and your life. Actively honoring them with words or actions further weaves their energy into the wellspring of energy that is maintained by your spiritual hearth. It may be enough for you to know and understand that they have had an effect upon you and who you are today. If you wish to honor them in a more structured fashion, try making an ancestor shrine. It doesn't have to be complicated; it can be as simple as placing a photograph of a relative who meant a lot to you near the spiritual heart of your home, or an item that belonged to them, or a small assembly of objects that you associate with your ancestors. Ancestors are not limited to biological relatives, either. Spiritual ancestors are people who have somehow shaped your outlook or way of life and whom you wish to honor or remember in some way. When calling upon the energy of your spiritual hearth you can wordlessly appeal to the ancestors as well, or speak aloud to them and ask for their support and blessing.

Here's a sample prayer to the ancestors for guidance or thanks:

Ancestors, thank you for being here with me and my family.
Guide us daily, and help us to make the right choices.
Be our strength and our comfort,
And help protect this home.
Thank you for your lives and your accomplishments.
Ancestors, we thank you.

At this point you may make an offering to them. Offerings are a sign of respect, not necessarily a sign of worship, and can be anything suitable. Ancestor honoring in many Neo-Pagan paths involves a small portion of something a specific ancestor enjoyed in life, but if you are calling upon your ancestors in general then something like a small thimbleful of tea, wine, or the food you are preparing is ideal.

If you don't know very much about your ancestors, try asking living relatives about their parents or grandparents. They may know stories that reveal hints about the ancestor's personality or activities. Genealogical research is another avenue you may wish to follow if the idea of ancestor energy particularly interests you. Learn as much as you can about ancestors, both biological and spiritual. Let them be a source of inspiration for you.

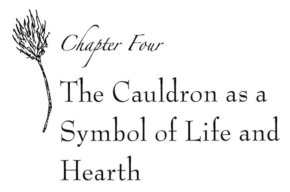

Chapter Four

The Cauldron as a Symbol of Life and Hearth

The cauldron is a symbol found in many cultures and folk tales. Closely associated with the hearth, the cauldron, along with the sacred fire, functions as a central symbol in the practice of hearthcraft, and a focal image in home-based spirituality.

The origin of the word "cauldron" comes from the Latin *caldarium*, meaning "hot bath," or *caldaria*, "cooking pot." And the cauldron is essentially a large metal pot, used for cooking over an open fire. The cauldron was (and still is, in many countries) an essential vessel in hearthside cooking. It has thus been commonly used throughout the ages until relatively recently. It was often set on a tripod rack or made with feet in order to set it in the embers or next to them, depending on what needed to be cooked. A curved handle was often also used, to suspend it from a hook in the fireplace over the fire.

At its most basic, the cauldron is associated with the everyday magic of cookery, the combination of ingredients and application of heat to create something new, which is nourishing, therapeutic, or supportive in some way. As a result of its practical physical use, the cauldron has become a symbol of abundance, source, warmth, nourishment, and transformation. Similar and related symbols are gourds and dippers, which share out the contents of some other container or source. The cornucopia is also a related symbol of abundance, prosperity, and nourishment.

Wells possess a similar physical structure, and have a physical source of liquid that represents healing or purification, whereas the cauldron's energy is derived from a mystical source. Like wells, cauldrons are connections to the Otherworld, a place of mysticism, the dead, enlightenment, and a realm of the divine, whence come inspiration and divine healing. The cauldron may also be seen as a symbol of initiation, wherein a symbolic death and rebirth are experienced. The cauldron is generally considered a feminine symbol, like most cups or bowl-shaped dishes. It is also associated with the element of water.

Transformation and transmutation are two of the most common themes associated with the cauldron in myth and story (see below). To transform is to undergo or initiate change in form or appearance. To transmute, however, is to change in *substance*, and is a term often used in chemistry or alchemy to describe the changing of one element into another. A cauldron can not only visibly alter something on the outside (transform), it can alter it on a very basic level, changing its very nature (transmute).

Symbolically, the cauldron offers us the opportunity to explore our inner self, the deep, dark well of our emotional nature. It can symbolize the repository of inner wisdom and hidden knowledge. Like the associations with the element of water in Western occult tradition, it can stand for the subconscious realm, the source of dreams, intuition, and healing.

The cauldron is sometimes associated with the Underworld, particularly in classical Greek and Roman iconology and belief (the cauldron suggest the shape of a cave, which was a place often sacred to chthonic goddesses), as well as the Otherworld that is often reached through a body of water in several cultural mythos.

Some prehistoric European burial sites feature urn-shaped vessels in which the deceased was placed, the body either gathered into a fetal position or cremated, and the vessel buried. This use of cauldron-shaped vessels for funereal purposes suggests the association of rebirth and transformation, another common association found in mythology (see below).

Cauldrons in Mythology

Cauldrons have figured largely in mythology, especially Celtic mythology. The traits of the separate mythological cauldrons tend to be synthesized by virtue of their similar root symbol, and thus one can encounter references to cauldrons that heal and feed and offer knowledge, all in one. Here are some of the most famous cauldrons and their stories.

The Cauldron of Cerridwen

Cerridwen is the Welsh goddess of grain and prophecy, generally perceived as a dark crone goddess. The cauldron she guards is the cauldron of Otherworld inspiration and divine knowledge. The most famous appearance of this cauldron is in the story of the birth of Taliesin, one of the most famous poets of the Celtic nation. Cerridwen set the boy Gwion Bach to stirring a potion she was brewing in her cauldron for a year and a day, intending the potion to bestow knowledge of all things past, present, and future upon her own son. On the final day three hot drops splashed from the cauldron onto Gwion Bach's thumb, and he instinctively lifted it to his mouth to cool it. With this act the potion's power transferred to him, rendering the rest of the brew useless. With the acquisition of such knowledge, Gwion Bach knew that Cerridwen would pursue him to punish him, and he fled, changing shape into first a hare, then a fish, then a grain of wheat to hide from her. Cerridwen did pursue him, changing shape to better hunt him as first a greyhound, then an otter, then a hen, swallowing the grain of wheat in triumph. Instead of consuming Gwion, however, Cerridwen found that she was pregnant, and gave birth to Gwion again. She sewed him in a leather bag and threw him into the sea, and he was found by a fisherman who named him Taliesin for his white brow.

The Cauldron of the Dagda

The Dagda is a father and fertility god of the Irish Tuatha Dé Danaan. His cauldron was known as Undry (or the Coire Anseasc) and possessed the power of producing plentiful, abundant food, capable of feeding an army without exhausting itself. A pertinent phrase often associated with the Dagda's cauldron is "no one ever went away from it hungry," an important concept when taken in the context of hearth and hospitality. In some versions of the Dagda's mythology, the cauldron only produces food in proportion with a man's merit. Some sources also attach the power of healing to the cauldron of the Dagda.

Also key to the precepts of hospitality, the Dagda's cauldron is said to be the resting place of the fiery-hot Spear of Lugh, one of the other Treasures of Ireland. This pairing demonstrates the peaceful and calming nature of the cauldron, containing the dangerous and war-like spear.

The Cauldron of Medea

Greek mythology tells us that Medea was a sorceress. When Jason came to Colchis on his quest to acquire the Golden Fleece, Medea, the daughter of King Aeëtes of Colchis, who kept the fleece, fell in love with him and promised to help him, in return for his promise to marry her and take her with him when he left. Jason agreed, and with Medea's help he passed each of the challenges. After other encounters they arrived in Iolicus, ruled by Jason's usurping uncle Pelias. Medea brought about his death by telling his daughters that she could revive and rejuvenate people by dismembering them and plunging them into her cauldron. She demonstrated this by dismembering an old goat or sheep and throwing the pieces into the cauldron, which was filled with herbs and a magical brew. A young living kid or lamb leapt out of the cauldron. The daughters agreed to do the same for their father, but Medea prepared the cauldron differently, filling it with water and only a few simple herbs. When the daughters dismembered Pelias and threw the pieces into the cauldron, without the brew of herbs and other preparations Medea had made, their plan failed and Pelias was dead.

Medea also used her cauldron at Jason's request to rejuvenate his father Aeson. Among other ritual activity, she combined herbs, flowers, seeds, stones, sand, frost, and parts of animals known for their vigor and long life. When the olive branch with which she was stirring it sprouted leaves and fruit, Medea knew the brew to be ready. She cut the throat of the old man and let all his blood run out, then poured the brew into his mouth and the wound on his throat. He grew forty years younger.

Medea was the granddaughter of Helios, the god of the sun, as well as the niece of sorceress Circe. Perhaps most importantly, she was a priestess of Hecate, a goddess of the underworld, and it was primarily from her that she drew her power. The cauldron is a critical element of Medea's rejuvenation magic, which suggests that it belongs to the tradition of cauldrons that restore life.

The Cauldron of Bran

From the annals of Welsh mythology comes the cauldron of Bran the Blessed, known as the Cauldron of Rebirth, which had the ability to resurrect the dead to life. Bran the Blessed gave it as a conciliatory gift to his new brother-in-law Matholwch, the King of Ireland, who married Bran's sister Branwen and whose horses were mutilated in anger by Bran's half-brother Efnisien. It was considered part of Branwen's dowry, and was taken back to Ireland when they returned.

Bran's cauldron has the ability to resurrect the dead. Immersing a man in the cauldron renders him alive and in peak physical condition by the next day, but those who are resurrected cannot talk. This is because they have been to the land of the dead, and may not speak of what they saw there to those who are still living. Unfortunately for Bran, the cauldron was used against him and his men when they later found themselves at war with the Irish: the king of Ireland repeatedly resurrected his slain warriors and returned them to battle. Bran's half-brother eventually broke the cauldron, sacrificing himself to do so.

The cauldron was said to have its origins in Ireland, under a lake. This further reinforces the rebirthing tradition, for the cauldron, like the lake, is a point of connection or interaction between the world of man and the Otherworld.

The Cauldron of Annwn

The quest for the Cauldron of Annwn is chronicled in the Welsh poem known as *Preiddeu Annwyn* (The Spoils of Annwyn), from the Book of Taliesin, which dates from somewhere between the ninth and twelfth centuries. Annwn is the Welsh Otherworld. One of the functions of the Celtic Otherworld is as a land of the dead. King Arthur and his companions travel to Caer Sidi, a fortress on an island ruled by the Lord of Annwn, and therefore they are essentially traveling to the land of the dead on this quest to obtain the cauldron belonging to the Lord of Death. The cauldron is enameled with flowers and studded with pearls or diamonds, cooled by the pure breath of nine maidens who protect it. One of the magical properties of this cauldron is that it will not boil the food of a coward, or one who is forsworn. It is so well protected that only Arthur and six other men return from this quest. They secure the cauldron, but at great cost.

A cauldron belonging to the Lord of Death can be assumed to be a cauldron like that of Bran the Blessed, one that rejuvenates or restores life.

Cauldron of Brigid

The Irish goddess Brigid (paralleled by Brid in Scotland and Brigantia in Britain, among others) is sometimes said to possess or carry a cauldron. This is a logical development from the extant Brigid myths, for not only is Brigid a goddess of inspiration, but she is a goddess of healing, associated with wells and water, and a goddess of fire and smithcraft. The cauldron is a water symbol, and is closely associated with fire for its connection to hearth and home, and also smithcraft, the method by which cauldrons are made.

Brigid is a goddess of three aspects, or alternately, three separate goddesses each called Brigid governing the realms of healing, poetry, and smithcraft. The smith aspect is known as Begoibne, which means "woman of the smithy." Begoibne was said to have a smithy under Croghan Hill in Ireland, where, among other things, she forged cauldrons, wherein the future was stored.

Odrerir, the Norse Cauldron of Inspiration

In Norse mythology, Odhinn drank magical blood from a cauldron to obtain wisdom.

He transformed himself into a serpent to drink all the poets' mead in the cauldron Odrerir. Odrerir is sometimes interpreted as the cauldron itself, as well as the mead of poetry inside it. The Prose Edda describes the blood of the god Kvasir, who was originally created from the saliva of all the gods, being blended with honey in the cauldron Odrerir by dwarves, and the resulting liquid was the mead drunk to transform the man drinking it into a skald, or scholar-poet. After bargaining for it by exchange of work and being denied his fair payment, Odhinn tricked the keepers of this cauldron using guile and disguise, and with three swallows drained the cauldron of the magical brew. In this way he became the god who dispenses inspiration to poets, in a sense liberating it from the giant Suttungr who jealously guarded it. This mead was also used by the Valkyries to restore life to the slain warriors who were been taken to Valhalla.

Exploring the Symbolism of the Cauldron

Looking at the myths above, the cauldron can be seen as a contained, controlled place for transformation. Think alchemy: the alchemical vessel is the crucible or alembic or flask in which dross is turned into gold (or, in a spiritual sense, the alchemical vessel is the mystical container for the soul or consciousness, which is what undergoes transformation in spiritual alchemy: this vessel is sometimes referred to as the womb, egg, or cup).

As a ritual vessel, the cauldron serves as a focus for transformative energies. It can represent the source, or the destination. It can symbolize wisdom, change, descent into the unknown, or rebirth. It's a wonderfully adaptive symbol.

It is very interesting to note that the cauldron dispenses both wisdom and nourishment in mythology. The parallel between the two suggests that wisdom nourishes the spirit, while food nourishes the body; a balance is created between the two. Equally, the spirit must be nourished by inspiration and wisdom, just as the body is nourished by food.

It is tempting to interpret the wisdom dispensed in cauldron myths as knowledge, possibly because knowledge can be quantified, whereas wisdom is something more elusive. Knowledge and wisdom are not the same thing. They complement one another, but they address different qualities. Knowledge is generally understood to be the technical aspect, while wisdom is the life experience absorbed and in turn applied. The *Oxford Dictionary* defines knowledge as "1: information and skills acquired through experience or education. 2: the sum of what is known. 3: awareness or familiarity gained by experience of a fact or situation." It defines wisdom as "the body of knowledge and experience that develops within a specified society or period." The distinction made between information or familiarity derived from experience, and the aggregate of experience within a large group, cultural or temporal, is significant.

Spiritual Work with a Cauldron

If there is one tool that I would recommend to anyone following a hearth and home-based spiritual path, it would be the cauldron. For all its symbolism and practical association with the hearth throughout history, the cauldron embodies so many of the goals and areas considered important in hearthcraft: abundance, nourishment, spiritual rejuvenation, introspection, and wisdom, to name only a few.

As hearthcraft is also about practicality, the cauldron isn't simply a symbol; it can be used in everyday activity as well, if you so desire. The modern kitchen cauldron is known as a Dutch oven, available with and without legs depending on indoor or outdoor use, and made of cast iron or enamelware.

If you acquire a cauldron solely for ritual or spiritual use, it doesn't have to be cast iron. While hearthcraft tends to be very practical and doesn't specify having a set of tools exclusively for ritual use, the cauldron may be one of those things you'd like to have two of: one heavy cast iron Dutch oven-type for cooking, and a smaller, lighter one for spiritual work and as a symbol on a shrine or altar. Lugging a twenty-five pound Dutch oven around can be a bit taxing.

You can use a tiny Dutch oven-style cast iron cauldron for ritual, or something else entirely. I have a beautiful hammered copper cauldron that I found at an antique market that's about ten inches in diameter that I use for most cauldron-based spiritual work, although if I make a needfire I use one of my cast iron cauldrons, as the heat and fire are better contained in those. China and ceramic urn-like dishes could also serve as symbolic cauldrons that are not to be used in conjunction with fire or heat.

When looking for a cauldron for spiritual work, keep in mind that you're going to want something that you can clean easily, as well as something that won't break or take up too much room; you may want to keep it out, on your altar or shrine for example, to use for offerings or to serve as a candleholder (a tea light in a small cauldron offers the image and feel of a needfire without the mess). Or you might use your cauldron as a focus for small honoring rituals, or as a visual focus during meditation.

Having a small symbolic cauldron is a practical way to incorporate the energies associated with it into your home, without having to store a huge cast iron pot somewhere. Small iron cauldrons, small enough to hold in the palm of your hand up to the size of two fists together, are easily placed somewhere about your workspace without cluttering it up.

Chapter 6 outlines creating a kitchen shrine. As a part of that shrine, you can use a small cauldron to hold a small amount of salt. Salt has been valued in many cultures for many reasons. The salt in your shrine or altar cauldron can be used for many things:

+ This salt can absorb negative energy in the space. If placed on the shrine with this intention, the salt will absorb negative energy, but don't use that salt for cooking, as representative of earth in a ritual, or for purifying anything.
+ Offer a pinch of this salt at the beginning or end of every day to the spirits of your hearth.
+ Add a pinch of this salt to your cooking and visualize it banishing anything negative that lingers, or as the catalyst that combines and binds the desired energies already present.

Be imaginative! The cauldron can be used in several different ways. Here are some suggestions to get you thinking about how you can involve the symbol of the cauldron into your spiritual practice and your daily work in and around the hearth.

+ Use your cauldron as a candleholder by slipping a tealight into it, or by filling it half full of sand or nonclumping kitty litter and placing a votive on top. Push the votive slightly into the sand so that it is steady before lighting it.
+ Put a layer of sand or nonclumping kitty litter in the bottom of your cauldron and place incense sticks in it, inserting the base of the stick firmly into the sand. Mound the sand around it if you have to in order to keep it upright. (If your incense

is the wooden-stick type, you can also snap some of the bare
stick off.)

+ Place a bit of food in your cauldron as an offering and place it
  on your shrine or altar.

+ Put a pinch of whatever herbs or spices you are using to season
  your food in the cauldron on the shrine or altar.

+ Place your cauldron in the center of your kitchen and visualize all the stagnant and negative energy spiraling into it from
  wherever it may be hiding—corners, behind the fridge, under
  the stove, under the sink . . .

+ When you need to calm yourself, set the cauldron on the
  table in front of you and breathe deeply to settle yourself.
  Visualize the darkness at the bottom of the cauldron being
  a portal to deep, soothing, cool energy. As you inhale, sense
  that energy flowing up to you. Feel the soothing energy fill
  you, relaxing tension, calming anger or fears. Do this until
  you feel calm again.

+ When you need to energize yourself, set the cauldron on the
  table in front of you and breathe deeply to settle yourself. Visualize the darkness at the bottom of the cauldron being a portal
  to a vibrant, joyful energy. As you inhale, sense that energy
  flowing up to you. Feel the energizing energy fill you, waken-
  ing your cells and energizing your body and mind. Do this
  until you feel ready to take on whatever task you have been
  preparing for.

+ Bring in flowers from your garden or that you have collected on
  a walk through your neighborhood. Place them in the cauldron
  on your altar or shrine. Remove them at the end of the day.

Using the Cauldron as a Meditative Focus

Use your cauldron as a meditative focus while saying a prayer or invocation. You can either gaze at the cauldron alone, or fill it with water and gaze into it. Here are some ideas for prayers to say before you meditate or to wrap a meditation session up. These are only suggestions; feel free to write and use your own.

CAULDRON PRAYER FOR ABUNDANCE

As a symbol of abundance, the cauldron really can't be beaten. Abundance encompasses things like prosperity, plenty of food, good friends, a healthy bank account, and so forth.

> *Blessed cauldron,*
> *I invoke through thee Undry,*
> *The great cauldron of the Dagda.*
> *Be for me a source of abundance,*
> *Nourishing energy, and strength.*

CAULDRON PRAYER FOR INSPIRATION

No matter what our métier—cooking, painting, writing, singing, parenting, answering phones, or driving a bus—there are days when we feel that everything we do is bland or unoriginal. If you feel like you need a bit of supportive inspiration from your spiritual hearth, try calling on Odhinn's cauldron of poet's mead for a creative pick-me-up.

> *Blessed cauldron,*
> *I invoke through thee the cauldron of Odhinn.*
> *Be for me a source of inspiration,*

That my work at hearth and in home be motivated by
Divine insight, handled with sensitive perception,
And carried out with poetry.

CAULDRON PRAYER
FOR SPIRITUAL RENEWAL

We all need to reinvent ourselves once in a while, especially if our lives feel stagnant, or you feel like you're getting nowhere. This prayer calls for figurative rebirth to help you get moving again. Remember: to be reborn, you need to give up what you currently have, so this prayer can initiate some changes in your life with which you may not be completely comfortable. It can be hard to give up ingrained ways of thinking, even if you know they're holding you back.

Blessed cauldron,
I invoke through thee the cauldron of Bran.
Wash me clean of what I no longer need,
And grant me new sight, new understanding,
And new energy to live my life.

CAULDRON PRAYER FOR WISDOM

Wisdom differs from knowledge in that it is the accumulation of enlightenment derived from putting knowledge into use, thereby gaining personal experience. Wisdom is what guides us in making moral or ethics-related decisions.

Blessed cauldron,
I invoke through thee the Cauldron of Cerridwen.

Be for me a source of wisdom,
That I may keep peace and equilibrium within my house,
And that all who step to my hearth know right from wrong.
Grant me insight, blessed cauldron,
And aid me in my daily decisions.

Caring for a Cast Iron Cauldron

It's important to know how to take care of a cauldron if you wish to have it around for a while. Enameled Dutch ovens are relatively easy to clean and care for, and so I'll focus here on the care of cast iron.

Before you use the cauldron as anything more than a visual symbol, it must be prepared and sealed, otherwise known as *seasoned*. New cast ironware is often a dull silvery color, but cast iron that has seen use is black. This does not affect the efficiency. Raw cast iron is very porous, and it has to be sealed before you use it. This is called seasoning the pot.

Make sure to wash your new cast iron pot well with soap and hot water before seasoning it, to remove any coating the production company may have put on it. If you've bought a secondhand cast iron cauldron at a flea market or garage sale and it's rusty, it can very easily be salvaged: scrub it down with a steel wool pad, then wash it well in hot soapy water and season it as below.

To season it, preheat the oven to 250–300 degrees Fahrenheit. Rub the cauldron inside and out with shortening or lard. (Vegetable or olive oil usually leaves a somewhat sticky residue, so avoid them.) Set the cauldron on a foil-lined baking sheet, and place the sheet in the preheated oven. After fifteen minutes, remove the cauldron with potholders and pour or wipe out any excess grease (it will have melted and collected in the cauldron). Replace in the oven and bake for one hour. Turn off the oven and allow the cauldron to cool inside.

To care for cast iron cookware, clean it while it is still warm by rinsing with very hot water and wiping it out with a paper towel. Make sure it is absolutely dry before you put it away. Some people say that you should never use dish soap, but the occasional wash with soap helps break down the food grease that may be left behind, which can go rancid. Never use a scrub pad, as it breaks down the seasoned surface. If you must, scrub the whole pot and then season it again (see above). Never allow the pot to sit with residue in it, or to stay wet after you rinse it, or it will rust.

An alternative to washing it in water is cleaning it with salt. Pour a 1–3 mm (just under a ¼ of an inch) layer of salt in the cast iron pot or pan. Heat it on the stovetop or in the oven at a very low temperature for at least a half hour. The salt will darken from the grease and dirt it absorbs. Remove from heat and allow the pan and salt to cool. Using a dry stiff brush (a brush designed for cleaning woks is good; under no circumstances use steel wool!) and scrub the salt off (remember, don't rinse it with water). Finish by wiping the surface down with paper towel or a soft cloth. The dry salt method ensures that you don't need to worry about making sure the cast iron is bone-dry before you store it, and there is no chance of rust.

To store cast iron cookware, line the inside of the pot with a sheet of paper towel to absorb any moisture and to reduce the chance of rust. If you have a lid for your cauldron, store it off the pot itself so as to allow the air to circulate freely around it; this also reduces the chance of rusting.

New Cauldron Blessing

When you acquire a cauldron, it's best to cleanse and purify it before use for either cooking or as a spiritual symbol or tool. You can adapt the basic purification ritual in Chapter 7, or create your own.

Once purified, you may say a blessing over the cauldron such as this one, or another of your choosing, or you may write one of your own.

> *Cauldron,*
> *Sacred symbol of rebirth,*
> *Of transformation and wisdom,*
> *Share with me your secrets and insight.*
> *May my life be touched by your energy*
> *As we work together.*
> *Cauldron, I welcome you into my home.*
> *Blessings upon you.*

If you like, you can sprinkle a few fresh or dried herbs inside it that represent blessing or welcome to you. (If you don't have any connection to herbs or sense an energy like this in any of them, check the appendix for a brief list of suggested herbs and their traditional associations.)

Your physical representation of the spiritual hearth or your kitchen altar or shrine (see Chapter 6) is the perfect place for your ritual cauldron to rest. As the cauldron is one of the focal symbols of hearthcraft, having it within sight while you work is ideal. Glancing at it now and again can help you refocus on whatever your spiritual purpose is: nourishing, loving, protecting, or whatever may be the theme of your work.

The Metals of Cauldrons

While early cauldron-like containers were made of dried and hollowed gourds or earthen clay, as humankind learned how to mine and work metal it became customary to form cooking vessels of the material, as they are placed in, near, or hung above fire in order to heat and cook the contents. In this way, a metal cauldron may be seen as associated with the symbol of fire, as fire is used to forge earth's metals, a symbol of water, as the element of water is used to cool it, and a symbol of earth, as the metals were extracted from the earth.

Even more correctly, however, the cauldron may be said to symbolize the interaction of these three elements, and thus be a symbol of transformation. The association of transformation is also derived from the alchemy of cooking that takes place inside it.

The metals commonly used to make cauldrons all have their own energies, which contribute to the overall energy within your kitchen. Being aware of what your kitchen tools are made of and the associations of their constituent elements can lend your spiritual work focus and awareness. This is a brief list of the common metals used for cauldrons and the associated energies; Chapter 8 looks at the energies of the metals commonly used for cauldrons and other kitchen tools in more depth.

- ✦ **Brass:** often used as a substitute for gold, therefore: prosperity; health; fire and sun energies; protection; attraction magic; deflecting of negativity.

- **Iron and Steel:** grounding; protection; deflecting magic and psychic energy; increase physical strength.
- **Copper:** revitalizing, refreshing, healing, kindness; fertility; love; beauty; harmony; friendship; peace; balancing outgoing and incoming energies, attracting money.
- **Aluminum:** travel; communication; mental activity; flexibility.
- **Tin and Pewter:** money; business success; fame and renown; legal issues.

Recipe: Cauldron Cookies

These fun little treats are a version of thumbprint cookies. Use the well in the center as the source for whatever you empower: nuts for abundance and fertility, and so forth. Cauldron cookies can be made and empowered with whatever energy you wish to associate with them, such as wisdom, abundance, or spiritual transformation. (See Chapter 9 for more information on the spiritual aspect of cooking and using food in a spiritual context.)

This recipe uses cocoa to make a chocolate cookie, which looks more like the traditional dark cauldron. If you wish to make a vanilla cookie, leave out the cocoa and add an extra spoonful or two of flour.

Alternatively, use any rich roll cookie recipe and don't add too much flour. Instead of rolling the dough out, roll it into small balls in your hands using a light touch, then place on a baking sheet and press your thumb into each ball. Dipping your thumb into icing sugar may help make the well.

Make sure you press your thumb into these cookies very deeply. If you only make a light impression the cauldron-like well is lost when the cookie bakes and rises slightly. Alternatively, you may bake them for four or five minutes, then press your thumb into the cookies, and bake them for the remaining time.

You will need:

+ 1 cup butter, softened
+ 1 cup brown sugar
+ 2 eggs
+ ¼ cup milk
+ 1 teaspoon vanilla
+ ⅔ cup cocoa
+ ½ teaspoon salt
+ 1 tsp baking powder
+ 2 cups flour

1. In a large bowl, cream the butter. Add the sugar and beat until fluffy. Add eggs and blend in one at a time. Add milk and vanilla, and blend carefully. Mix well.
2. In another bowl, whisk together flour, cocoa, baking powder, and salt. Fold into the butter mixture carefully, then mix until well blended.
3. Cover bowl with plastic wrap and refrigerate for at least one hour, or until firm enough to handle.
4. Heat oven to 350 degrees F. Roll dough into one-inch balls. Place on lightly greased baking sheets. Press thumb deeply but

gently in center of each ball. (Dusting your hands with icing sugar may help prevent the dough from sticking too much while rolling the balls and pressing your thumb into them.)

5. Bake for 10–12 minutes, or until set. Cool slightly on baking sheet, then remove from sheet to finish cooling on a wire rack. Cool completely before filling.

Filling suggestions:

+ Jam
+ Whipped cream
+ Lightly crushed berries, sprinkled with a bit of sugar (let this mixture sit for at least an hour before filling the cookies)
+ Frosting
+ Nut butter

If you want to carry the cauldron theme further, use thin strips of licorice candy as handles.

Chapter Five

Hearth Deities and Spirits

There are a multitude of deities and spirits associated with the hearth in every culture, demonstrating the spiritual importance of this area. The concept of hearth and home are so completely intertwined that deities associated with one are generally associated with the other. Here, then, is a sample of various hearth and domestic deities from several different cultures. It is by no means exhaustive, nor are the entries complete.

Hestia

The Greek goddess of the hearth, Hestia was the deity to whom offerings were made before any other. The saying "Hestia comes first" points to how entrenched she was in the lives and spiritual practice of these people. The Homeric Hymn to Hestia XXIX says,

Hestia, in the high dwellings of all, both deathless
gods and men who walk on earth, you have gained an everlasting
abode and highest honour: glorious is your portion and your
right. For without you mortals hold no banquet, where one
does not duly pour sweet wine in offering to Hestia both first
and last.

Despite her first-among-equals position, Hestia is rarely referred to in myth; there are very few stories involving her, and her behavior is passive when she does appear. She seems to be more of an unembodied ideal than an enfleshed deity as the other Olympians are presented in story. This does not mean that she did not play a significant role in the lives of the Greeks. On the contrary: because Hestia was ever-present in the form of the home hearth as well as the public hearth, she was understood to be so entrenched in daily life that stories painting her as larger than life were unnecessary.

One of the three original Greek goddesses of the first generation of Olympians, Hestia was considered a virgin goddess, not beholden or subservient to any other person or deity. As a hearth goddess she was associated with the baking of bread and the preparation of meals. Identified also with the sacred flame, she was thereby connected to offerings, and received a portion of every offering made to other gods.

Despite not having a formal temple, Hestia was honored by a public altar in the city hall, or *prytaneum*, where an eternal flame was kept lit. Just as the hearth represents the spiritual heart of the private home, the public hearth dedicated to Hestia was considered the heart of the city. When a new town was founded, embers from the public hearth would be carried to kindle the fire in the public hearth of the new municipality, transporting Hestia's essence and protection to bless the new settlement. Likewise, family members establishing a new home elsewhere would bring embers from their home hearth to their new hearth.

Hestia preserves the sanctity of the private home, keeping it a refuge and a place of spiritual renewal. The hearth was considered the spiritual heart of the private home, and the fire in it was not extinguished. If it did go out, rituals of purification and renewal were necessary to relight it. As Hestia was the essence of the home, formalized worship was effectively nonexistent; everyone honored her on an individual basis. Hestia is an example of how holy the hearth and hearthfire were considered, and how sacred the home as temple was for a family.

Her presence is symbolized by a flame burning on the hearth or altar. Hestia is rarely portrayed in iconology, for she is instead understood to be the flame itself. If portrayed, however, she is sometimes shown with a flowering branch, a kettle or cauldron-shaped pot, or a torch.

It is very interesting that Hestia is seen as an old maid or homebody, which generally have pejorative or dismissive associations in modern society. It should be remembered that older women were considered wise and experienced, and honored in ancient societies.

Vesta

The Roman cognate of Hestia is Vesta, and while performing a similar function and position, Vesta is not precisely equal to the Greek goddess of the hearth. A major difference is that Vesta's worship was formalized, and an order of priestesses served her in formal temples.

Vesta's temple housed an eternal flame that symbolized the life and safety of the city of Rome itself. It was guarded and watched over by a group of priestesses dedicated to the service of Vesta called the Vestales, or Vestals. These priestesses swore to devote their lives to Vesta, and thus pledged celibacy for thirty years in order to devote all their energy and time to serving the goddess, giving rise to the descriptive name "the Vestal virgins."

Vesta's sacred fire was relit every first of March. A sample of the fire was taken and kept safe in a container. After cleaning the hearth, the fire was lit again from the embers kept safe from the original fire. In this sense, the eternal flame was truly eternal, the essence of the previous year's flame and all the years before it being passed on in the embers to the new fire. The remains of sacrificial fires in the temple were also considered sacred, and the ashes were collected and stored under the temple until the yearly procession to the Tiber where they were thrown in. Vesta's festival was known as the Vestalia, celebrated from June 7 to June 15.

Like Hestia, her presence is symbolized by a flame burning on an altar or the hearth of the home. Iconology depicts her with a javelin and/or an oil lamp.

Brigid

The much-loved Irish goddess of the home, Brigid is known by other names such as Brid and Brigantia in regions that later became Scotland and Britain. Brigid has three aspects: a smith, a healer, and a poet. She is strongly associated with the element of fire, and to a lesser degree with the element of water.

All three of her aspects have bearing on the practice of hearth-craft. The smith works with the element of fire, which is, like the cauldron in the previous chapter, an agent of transformation and transmutation. The smith also makes tools, many of them for home and homestead use such as cauldrons, hooks, nails, hearth sets (the tools for tending and cleaning the fireplace), fire irons (the metal supports that hold logs and other fuel to be burned) and so forth. Brigid's healing aspect focuses on restoring and maintaining health, one of the areas hearthcraft also touches. And the poet's inspiration is often symbolized by a flame.

Brigid has survived into the modern age as a Catholic saint, whose areas of influence are certainly hearth and home related. She is the patron saint of livestock such as sheep and cattle, dairy products such as milk and butter and workers in the dairy industry (including milk-maids and dairy maids), children, poultry farmers, midwives, poets, and blacksmiths. Her many associations with house and home make her a very popular goddess with whom to work.

Brigid was worshipped, both as goddess and later as a saint, by a circle of nineteen priestesses or nuns who tended an eternal flame. On the twentieth day the flame was said to survive without anyone visibly tending it, leading to the belief that the goddess herself tended the flame that day.

Tsao Wang

Tsao Wang is the Chinese god of the hearth, also known as the kitchen god. An image of Tsao Wang (and sometimes his wife) is kept in the kitchen, usually above or near the stove, symbolic of the god's presence. Incense is burned in his honor regularly, or other offerings made. Tsao Wang is said to keep watch over the family through the year, and his wife records the good things said by each family member. The week before Chinese New Year, Tsao Wang is said to leave the hearth to report to heaven on the family's doings. Because a good report is desired, it is customary to offer sticky sweets to Tsao Wang, as well as wine and money in order to make his journey comfortable. The report Tsao Wang makes will determine if the family will be assigned good or bad luck for the coming year.

During the period when Tsao Wang is gone the image is turned to face the wall, or if it is paper it is burned. Before Tsao Wang returns the house must be cleaned thoroughly to banish any ill luck or negative energy that is present, with every member of the family or resident of the house helping to ensure good fortune in the coming year. (The house must not be cleaned in the days immediately following the New Year, or the good luck may be lost.) The image is then turned right way round again to symbolize his return, or a new image brought in to replace the one that was burned. A special meal is then prepared to welcome him back to the hearth.

China and Japan have several customs and traditions surrounding hearth and home, often revolving around honoring family, ancestors, and hearth spirits. As they can't all be included here, you could do your own independent research to explore how highly they respect the spirits associated with the sacred space of home, and the various traditions ranging from feasts and specific foods to offerings and festivals.

The Way of the Hedge Witch

Kamui-fuchi

Kamui-fuchi is a Japanese goddess of the hearth, originally from the Ainu people. Her name means Rising Fire Sparks Woman, and she is symbolized by the flame in the hearth. Legend has it that she never leaves this home, and therefore the fire is never allowed to die. She is the major overseer of the household, but as she does not leave her place there are other household spirits that report to her. She guards the home, and also dispenses justice in domestic affairs.

In Ainu tradition, the hearth is also the dwelling place of the ancestors, locating them in the heart of the household. The hearth fire was also seen as a doorway through which the family could communicate with the spirit world.

Kamado-no-Kami

Kamado-no-Kami is the Japanese god of the cooking fire, or stove and oven. Like Tsao Wang, Kamado-no-Kami exists in every home simultaneously. He, too, is a god of purification; however, as the fire itself is believed to be easily polluted, there are rites for purification of the fire or oven itself as well. Shrines to him are maintained in many kitchens to both help with the daily fire and restrain its dangerous nature.

Kamado is also the word for a cooking pot in some regions of Japan, and so this deity can also be associated with cauldrons. Kamado-no-Kami is one of the set of fire deities (*hi-no-kame* or *hinokame*), and his sphere of protection extends from the hearthfire to the whole household and the food prepared within it. The term "kami" is the general term for spirit, and for it to be an official part of his name signifies how central Kamado-no-Kami is to the culture. Koujin-Sama is the syncretic Shinto-Buddhist deity of the kitchen and the cooking stove, and an analog of Kamado-no-Kami.

Gabija

The Lithuanian goddess of the earth fire, Gabija (also Gabieta, Gabeta) was perceived as a protector of the household. The hearth fire was believed to be a purifying energy that would defend the house from unclean people and creatures. Tradition dictated that the hearth fire be extinguished and ritually relit every midsummer. When a fire was laid, a cup of water or beer would be left as an offering for Gabija. When the fire was banked each night, the woman of the household would pray to Gabija for good fortune and safety for the family. As in the cult of Hestia, a bride would take embers from her family's hearth and use them to lay a fire in her new home. Some sources say that a pinch of salt would be tossed into the fire as an offering. Another form of this goddess, Gabjaua, was associated with grain crops and brewing.

Ertha

A domestic deity from Northern Europe, Ertha is associated with earth and abundance, fate, peace, as well as domestic life. She is a Germanic version of Mother Earth. In some myths, she is the mother of the three Norns, triplet sisters who control fate and destiny. Divination was often a hearthside activity, and fire is often used as a divination tool, so this association makes sense. Ertha is said to have flown through the smoke of the kitchen fire to leave small presents for each member of the family at the winter solstice, a practice very similar to the activity we assign to Santa Claus and Father Christmas.

Frigga

One of the main female deities in Norse mythology, Frigga (also known as Frigg in some sources) is a domestic goddess in the true sense of the term. Wife to Odinn, she is considered a goddess of marriage and love, fertility, motherhood, household management and all the domestic skills. Far from being subservient, she is powerful and shares Hlidskjalf, Odinn's high seat that looks out over the world, the only other god permitted to sit in this throne-like chair. She possesses the power of prophecy, although she keeps the knowledge of the future to herself. These last two facts suggest how very powerful she is, and how much information she possesses about the land and areas under her rule. With this knowledge she can best arrange and perform her tasks, maintaining an environment that is calm, well-managed, and supportive for those in her care.

Frigga has companions and attendants, all associated with domestic-related virtues and paths. Eir is the goddess of healing; Hlín is a goddess of protection; Gná is a goddess of messages and communication; and Fulla is another fertility goddess.

The symbols commonly associated with Frigga are the spinning wheel and the distaff, or drop spindle. Mistletoe is a plant commonly associated with her, a plant that possesses healing, fertility, and protective powers.

Bes

The dwarf Egyptian god of protection, Bes was often depicted on household items, associating him with the general protection of the household. He is a defensive fighter god, protecting the family both inside the house and outside it, and also a god who drives away ill fortune.

Household Spirits

A household spirit is a guardian that defends the home or some specific part of it, or the family members. These spirits are not formal deities or mythological figures; rather, they are unique to the hearth and family. They may be related to the ancestors, or they may be spirits of place. Household spirits are honored within the home, and often represented by small figures or paintings, or engravings on household items. Household spirits are generally acknowledged by the family and are given offerings of various food and/or drinks, or honored in other ways. In general, the cultural associations made with these spirits are of protection of the home, protection of family members, and prosperity.

The Roman cult of the hearth and family is an excellent example of how household spirits function within daily life and spiritual activity of the family. An example of household spirits are the *lares familiarius* of ancient Rome (singular *lar*). The *lares* were spirits associated with different places or activities. The *lar familiarius* (literally a "family guardian") was a household god or spirit associated with an individual family home. A small shrine known as a *lararium* was provided for the lares, part shrine and part home for these spirits, appearing variously as a niche in a wall, a wall cupboard, or a freestanding cupboard. The lararium was placed near the hearth, the central focus of the home, or in an entryway, sometimes co-occupying or beside a shrine to Vesta. Small statues of the lares were placed in and around the home to protect it, sometimes on the roof or other high places. The lar was an essential part of family life, in both day-to-day events and formal family functions. If individuals within the family honored the lar, then the spirit would protect each of them and ensure they had good fortune. If an individual did not properly honor the spirit, then he or she would be ignored and denied the spirit's aid.

The lares had their own festival called the Compitalia, celebrated around the fourth of January. The Compitalia is associated with the concept of crossroads, an interesting symbol when you consider how much power the lar held to help or hinder a family. Some records suggest that there were different lares for different zones of the house, such as the doorways, the hearth, and so forth. The *penates*, for example, were originally spirits of the pantry and storerooms, who when properly honored would ensure that the family was prosperous and always had enough to eat. In Virgil's *Aeneid*, Aeneas pauses to take the small figures of the hearth gods with him as he flees. This action suggests that wherever the hearth gods are, home is as well. Taking the physical representation and focus for the spirits along with him symbolizes transporting the entire ancestry and culture as he seeks a new home and founds the new city.

While the lares were literally spirits of place, remaining in the house when a family moved and protecting everyone within it regardless of station or kinship, the *manes* were the actual spirits of family ancestors and beloved dead. *Di manes* can be translated as meaning "the good ones" or "kindly ones." These spirits protected the family itself, not the house or household servants.

Shinto, the native religion of Japan, has as one of its tenets an honor for family and tradition. A Shinto home will usually have a small shrine or altar called the *kamidama* (a "god shelf" or "spirit shelf"), placed high on a wall in a central living area of the home. This altar is often a small shelf, or a small house-like structure or façade, set up to house ritual objects. Traditionally, the five offerings made at a kamidana are rice, sake (rice wine), water, salt, and evergreen branches or incense. The tiny set of objects used on the altar for these offerings are known as *shinki* and include white ceramic vases for the evergreen branches, flasks with lids to hold blessed sake, a small dish for rice, a flask with a lid for blessed water, a small dish for salt, and a low wooden platform or tray on which to display the shinki set, as well as miniature replicas of the lamps found in large formal shrines. Before any offering is made, the individual must wash her hands well. While the kamidana is not dedicated solely to the *kamadogami* or Shinto hearth gods, it is certainly one of the kinds of spirits honored there. Creating a small location such as this in which to focus your honoring of your own household spirits and ancestors is another way to explore the spirituality of the home and to honor it. (See Chapter 3 for more information about constructing a physical representation of the spiritual hearth, and Chapter 6 for more information on constructing a kitchen shrine.)

European cultures have also retained certain house spirits that have been encoded in folk tales, but are still referred to in modern times and remembered in cultural tradition. These spirits are generally male, often hairy, human-shaped but in smaller proportion or miniature stature, and are generally benevolent unless provoked by disrespect or open recognition. If one of these household spirits is associated with your cultural ancestry, you may think about inviting one to take up residence in your home. Just make sure to treat it properly!

- ✦ **Brownie (Scotland, England):** A familiar household spirit, the brownie is generally described as a small brown human, dressed in tattered clothes or in nothing at all. Sometimes there are minor physical differences from humans, such as webbed hands, missing fingers, or a flat nose. Brownies are perhaps the most helpful domestic spirits one can possibly have, helping and supporting in every possible domestic activity. It is essential that a brownie receive no other sign of appreciation than a dish of rich milk or fresh bread or cake left out for him, or the brownie will leave forever. Spoken thanks and new clothes are especially forbidden. Criticism of any kind is also forbidden, for the brownie will take offense and create a complete mess while destroying household goods. Some brownies also protect their households, or use playful trickery to expose household members who are lazy and skimp on their chores!

- ✦ **Boggart (England, North Country region):** Boggarts can be either helpful or malevolent spirits. They do not tend to have physical forms, although stories exist wherein specific boggarts take physical form to torment or mislead people. Boggarts are mischievous and like playing tricks, often exhibiting poltergeist-like behavior. Benevolent boggarts are brownie-like in their behavior and will help out with domestic tasks. Like a brownie, however, it must be treated well, or it can and will display destructive behavior. The Welsh bwca is a form of brownie.

+ **Hob (England):** The hob functions much like a brownie, but instead of providing general help he focuses on one specific task. The name refers to the flat part of a range or stovetop, or the flat place or shelf by a hearth where pans could be heated or kept warm. The same cautions regarding thanking and criticizing brownies applies to hobs. The hob can be attached to a specific house or piece of land, or a family, following them if they move. The hob is also known as a hobgoblin, which is sometimes considered a nature spirit or confused with the malicious goblin.

+ **Domovoi (Russia):** The domovoi is a helpful household spirit much like the English brownie. They are described as little old men with gray beards who live under or near the hearth, or sometimes the threshold of the house. While "dom" means house, the domovoi is linked to the family and will move with them when properly invited. Domovoi sometimes help with chores, but their primary focus is on protecting the house and the residents. A portion of the evening meal is always set aside for him, and the family never refers to him by name, only by a nickname such as "old grandfather." Like most household spirits, the domovoi must be kept happy, or the family risks ill fortune and suffering from poltergeist-like activity.

+ **Tomte (Sweden):** The tomte or tomtar is a house spirit, again male and ranging from a few inches to two feet tall, who is attached to a piece of land upon which a house has been built. The tomte's preferred food is porridge, often with a pat of butter on top, served to him on Christmas morning. The presence of the tomte ensures a smoothly run and prosperous household, sometimes at the expense of neighbors who lose grain or supplies to the tomte as he works to keep the household under his guardianship successful. The tomte is gifted with incredible strength far beyond what one would imagine. In Finland this spirit is known as the Tonttu. Images of the tomte as a small man with a white beard and tall pointed red hat are often seen around Christmas.

✦ **Nisse (Denmark, Norway):** A brownie-like household spirit who likes a quiet and orderly household, the nisse or nis works on household chores at night. Like the tomte he may stealthily acquire goods and supplies from neighbors to supplement his household's stock of goods. The nisse's preferred method of being thanked is to be left a bowl of porridge with a pat of butter. His special skill is speed.

✦ **Kobold (Germany):** A kobold is a household spirit who could manifest as human, animal, fire, or household object. Similar to brownies and other household spirits, they are most frequently described as humans between two and four feet tall. Kobolds either live under the hearth or in a less-trafficked area such as a woodshed or attic. They finish what chores have been left undone when the family has gone to bed, keep pests away, and help the family maintain an abundance of food and good fortune. As is customary, the kobold and his efforts must be respected, or the family risks losing its services and suffering dreadful misfortune, illness, and hardship. Like the Roman household spirits and gods, German peasants carved effigies and small figures of kobolds to protect their houses. There are other kinds of kobolds in German mythology as well, specifically those who dwell in mines and those who work aboard ships.

Although not considered gods in a real sense, these more mischievous household spirits had to be kept content in order to avoid ill fortune or obstacles in daily life. In some cases, keeping a spirit content meant not acknowledging it, as in the case of the brownie.

Offerings to Household Spirits

Offerings are a way of honoring your chosen principals, guardians, or concept of the sacred. The term "offering" suggests that what you are giving to the entity you are honoring is in some way precious to you. Anything can be an offering.

Every house will have different spirits, and they will all have different personalities, likes, and dislikes. For example, I have a friend whose household spirits were often particularly helpful after she bought them a double-double coffee (two cream and two sugars) from the local coffee shop and left it on the altar for them. Food is a simple offering, and one that is commonly made throughout the world. In Japan, for example, the practice of scattering rice in the four corners and in the center of the site as an offering to a kami or god is called *sanku*. The basic food offerings such as sake, salt, and water are called *shinsen*, although an offering may be of any food beyond these as well, cooked or otherwise.

Many traditional offerings tie in to the basic foods prepared at the hearth, especially bread and porridge. A simple way to honor your house spirits is to leave a portion of the meal you are serving to your own family aside for them, either on your kitchen shrine or in another place. The amount depends on what you can spare or what you think the spirit would appreciate. Excess might suggest to the spirit that you have more than enough and do not need help; too little may offend it. A spoonful may be enough. Leave the offering overnight, and dispose of what is left the next morning. While it may not seem as if any has been consumed, the argument is often made that spirits absorb the energy of an offering, and they certainly are aware of the action and appreciate the respect and acknowledgement thus demonstrated.

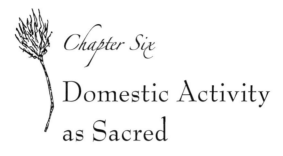

Chapter Six

Domestic Activity as Sacred

In today's homes, often the only place that approximates a hearth is the kitchen. This isn't surprising when you consider that the kitchen plays a central role in everyday life, being the place where food is prepared and eaten. Home-based spirituality incorporates domestic activity of all kinds, and most domestic activity is based or originates in the kitchen, so it makes sense to establish a spiritual element there.

It can be hard to shake the mindset drilled into North American culture by the technological improvements in the mid- to late-twentieth century. Advertising dating from the 1950s and 1960s repeatedly targeted wives and mothers as people who deserved to spend more time out of the kitchen to live a "real" life. Inventions and prepackaged foods to shorten time spent in the kitchen and reduce energy devoted to kitchen- and domestic-related activity have somehow led us to believe that the kitchen is a place where we ought not to be. We don't have to do that old stuff any more, prepackaged and processed foods whisper to us as we walk the aisles of our local grocery markets; we've advanced beyond an inferior and less desirable past.

In a way, this is sad. It suggests that the kitchen is a place to avoid, a place where we ought to spend the least amount of time possible. We have come to regard food preparation and domestic activity as things that have to be done before we get to do the other rewarding things in life. As a friend said to me the other day, "We have to learn to understand that running a household is not only work, it's valid work. It's not something that gets squeezed in after six o'clock. It's not taking away from other things if we do it between nine and five." And she's right. The feminist revolution of the latter half of the twentieth century succeeded in opening the workplace to women, but unfortunately, in so doing it suggested that domestic management was somehow inferior to work done elsewhere. When establishing a home-based spirituality, it's important to examine your feelings about the kitchen and the work done there. Even if you choose another room or area to be your symbolic hearth, the function of the kitchen doesn't change, and so much of domestic activity is based there that your feelings about it will certainly influence home-based spiritual work.

The kitchen hasn't always been a separate room in the house. Originally it was nothing more than a cooking fire brought indoors, with the other shelter-based activity carrying on around it. As the kitchen evolved into a specialized area it became its own room, with separate areas for storage of food, equipment, and activity. The room became further separated into a hot kitchen and cold kitchen where space permitted, the hot kitchen containing the fireplace and hearth for roasting meats and making hot foods, and the cold kitchen a place of lower temperature where foods such as pastry, jellied foods, and dairy were kept or prepared.

Older kitchens were larger than the ones we use today, as they encompassed a wide variety of pursuits. Apart from cooking, activities such as eating, washing laundry, taking baths, candle making, spinning and weaving, sewing, food preserving in all forms, nursing the sick, childcare, lessons, and countless other pursuits all took place in the kitchen of the average home.

As the twentieth century saw the invention of time- and labor-saving devices, the kitchen began to shrink in size as less time was spent there and activities were relocated to specific activity-associated areas. The trend in downsizing began to reverse in the late twentieth century. Today's kitchen designs feature layouts that returned to an open-plan arrangement, allowing families to congregate in a larger room and share time together. There's a reason why we see kitchens being designed with large work or relaxation spaces adjacent and open to the actual kitchen area, and computer nooks in the kitchen itself. With less time spent in the home in general, families seek to make the most of their time together. It makes sense that families come together in the kitchen or adjacent open-plan rooms while a meal is being prepared.

Kitchens have always changed in size and equipment according to the needs of the era. And yet throughout it all, they are continually associated with domesticity and the heart of the home. The kitchen is a key communal area in most homes: It is a meeting place, a social area, a point of communication, a place where food is stored, prepared, and consumed. All the related equipment for these activities is stored here as well.

The kitchen is the one room in the house that sees a constant stream of activity. It is seen less so nowadays, what with the use of appliances that can store and prepare food in a fraction of the time once necessary, as well as the widespread use of preprepared and prepackaged food. Historically, however, the kitchen was in constant use. It served as the headquarters of the home, a staging place for maintaining the running of the household: it was the location of the pantry, and adjacent to the storage place of foodstuffs; it was where the cooking fire resided, which required constant supervision; it was where food preparation and preservation took place, and in many cases it was where the food was consumed as well.

Don't dismiss this chapter if your physical analog or your spiritual hearth is located elsewhere in your home. The function the kitchen serves in a family's everyday life links it strongly to your hearth and home-based spirituality.

In terms of hearthcraft, the kitchen as a place of physical nourishment is a logical parallel to the spiritual center of your home. If this is true for you, then setting up an altar or shrine to represent your spiritual hearth in the kitchen makes perfect sense. If your kitchen is poorly laid out or a place of stress for you, thinking about what creates an atmosphere more conducive to a spiritual environment or setting up an altar or shrine there can help you redirect, purify, or otherwise make the energy of your kitchen more appealing, and make your experience there a happier and more rewarding one. If you hate your kitchen, anything that might help should be tried at least once!

If in the end the kitchen is just absolutely not the heart of your home, no matter how you look at it, don't fight it; go with wherever you feel drawn to. Do your best to open yourself to the spiritual aspect of the work done in the kitchen by employing some of the techniques in this book.

Kitchen Altars and Shrines

While your entire kitchen is and can be sacred space (see the discussion on sacred space in Chapter 2), creating a defined location within the kitchen that serves as sacred space can help you focus on the spiritual aspect of hearthcraft while using the existing space in your kitchen in a practical fashion. These defined places or zones provide you with a touchstone of sorts, a place or thing that you can use to represent the greater whole.

The term *altar* can evoke the concept of something formal and untouchable. In Neo-Pagan usage an altar generally means simply a physical space used for magical work or worship. It provides a place of focus. A *shrine* is generally a specific site set up to honor an entity or principle. Do you have to figure out which you're using in hearthcraft? No; the word isn't important. A lot of the time your altar/shrine will be a place that symbolizes or otherwise represents your connection with or to deity, or your concept of the sacred. What you call it isn't important. In this book, both words are used to mean the same thing: the special spot in your kitchen (or elsewhere) that you have chosen to house meaningful objects and symbols, which stimulates and supports your ongoing spiritual practice. If you intend to use it as a place to display meaningful objects connected with a hearth deity or house spirit and as a place to leave offerings, it is probably a shrine. If you intend to use it primarily as a place for some sort of eternal flame and as somewhere to put short-term spiritual items as you work with them over a short-term basis, including magical items such as sachets or empowered symbols and objects, it's probably an altar. Altars can be designated as more active and projective, whereas shrines tend to be more passive and receptive. Does it matter if you can't define or clearly separate what you're setting up or what you intend to do at them? No. Empires will not crumble, nor will your communication to the Divine be cut off. It also doesn't matter if you set one up and it slowly takes on the characteristics of the other, or if you set up one place to do double duty as both. In the end, what you're doing is creating a place to serve as a physical point of reference for your spiritual work, an interface for your communication with the Divine.

An altar or shrine is a created sacred space, an area set apart to honor a concept or force, a deity or spirit, or to represent your connection to the Divine. They can represent emotions, commitments, or just about anything you desire or require. A space such as this in the hearth, the spiritual heart of the home, stands as a formal physical representation of the *spiritual* hearth. It provides a "home" for the symbolic hearth. A formal physical representation of the hearth makes it easier for you to visualize it and interact with it. People usually find it easier to work with a tangible representation than an abstract concept, no matter how strongly we may feel that abstract concept's presence. We like to mark the places we consider sacred in some way, partially in honor of what we feel is sacred, but also to remind ourselves of that sanctity, and to create an analogy in the physical world.

Is it essential to have a kitchen altar or shrine? Well, yes and no. You can certainly cultivate and manage a spiritual environment without one, but it's a lot easier to do if you have a physical place where you can focus your attention now and again. A place where you can collect certain special things that symbolize or remind you of your connection to the sacred principles in your life is a unique thing. It's simply easier for most people to have a physical representation of what's going on in their heads and spirits. Human beings are somewhat magpie-like in that shiny things attract them and make them feel good. It's gratifying to have a designated place to burn candles or incense, or leave tiny offerings to your house spirits or the universe in thanksgiving, or to put the first leaf of autumn or violet of spring.

A kitchen shrine or altar doesn't need to be something large. And that's a good thing, because space in a kitchen is generally already at a premium. Some may already consider their counters or stovetop to be sacred space, and that's fine. But one of the benefits of creating a single focal point in the kitchen to serve as a shrine is that it keeps your spiritual or magical-related work off your main everyday workspaces. Most of us already wish we had more workspace in our kitchens, so keeping extra things off the counter is good if you want to be doing something spiritual that isn't directly incorporated into your food preparation. A separate altar also keeps potentially nonconsumable materials away from places where food is prepared. And finally, it keeps things such as smoldering incense or burning candles and oil lamps safely out of harm's way. There's no rule that stipulates only one such space per kitchen or home, either. If you want to set up two or more, do it! If you create a physical representation of the spiritual heart of your home, adding a kitchen shrine doesn't take away from that physical hearth.

There are things to consider when you design a kitchen shrine or altar. First of all, the location should be somewhere accessible, yet out of the way in order to protect the objects upon it. There's a lot of activity in the kitchen, and you don't want your shrine area to be continually disturbed; there are also the safety issues mentioned above. You do need to get to it on a semi-regular basis, though. Places you can consider using include:

+ above the doorframe (a narrow shelf is ideal)
+ a wall shelf
+ a series of narrow shelves running about a foot below the ceiling (plate rails, for example)
+ on the back of the stove, along the top of the back plate (you may need to set a board on top of it to provide a wider surface, and remember that if your fuses are located there, the shrine and its contents will have to be moved to access them)
+ hanging baskets (wire or wicker; the three-tiered baskets make an interesting multilevel shrine)
+ a hanging pot rack (I place bunches of dried flowers and other natural objects on top)

Here are some suggestions for items you may wish to include on your shrine or altar:

+ something to represent your connection to your ancestors
+ something to represent your household or hearth spirits

- something to represent a hearth diety with whom you have a special connection or resonance, cultural or otherwise
- something to represent the four elements (earth, air, fire, and water) or simply fire as a symbol of the spiritual hearth

Creating Figures for Your Shrine

Rather than use found objects for your shrine, you can make images to represent the guardians or deities that you feel guide you in your kitchen. Or you can make representations of those entities and energies you wish to invoke in your hearth to attract more of the same, or to be guiding lights.

For this project, you can use self-hardening clay, also known as air-drying, which does not require baking to set, or heat-dried clay or other modeling substance. Work on a surface that is flat, and cover your surface with plastic or newspaper to protect it from the clay.

Before you begin, decide what kind of shape or figure you wish to sculpt or form. It doesn't have to be a literal portrayal of the spirit or deity you feel drawn to; allow yourself to be inspired. Perhaps spend a few minutes with a pencil and paper doodling shapes or ideas for the figure. If you are making a figure to represent an abstract principle, again let your inspiration and instinct guide you.

The mint in this project is associated with abundance; the lavender is associated with peace; the cloves are associated with purification; the basil is associated with harmonious domestic management; the rosemary is associated with protection; the sage is associated with purification; and the salt is associated with purification and prosperity. These were chosen for their general association with common themes in the practice of home-based spirituality. If there are other herbs whose energies are more appropriate to your chosen spirits or goal, use them instead.

You will need:

- ✦ Self-hardening or oven-dried clay (about the size of your fist), color of your choice
- ✦ 1 pinch dried mint
- ✦ 1 pinch dried lavender
- ✦ 1 pinch ground cloves (or one whole clove)
- ✦ 1 pinch dried basil
- ✦ 1 pinch dried rosemary
- ✦ 1 pinch dried sage
- ✦ 1 pinch salt
- ✦ Small dish for herbs
- ✦ Tools to work the clay (toothpick, chopstick, skewer, etc.)
- ✦ Candle, candleholder
- ✦ Matches or lighter
- ✦ Small dish of rice or salt

1. Take a moment to sit quietly and clear your mind. Take three deep breaths, releasing as much physical and mental tension as possible with each exhalation.
2. Light the candle, saying:

Sacred flame,
Bless my work with your light.

3. Take the clay and begin to knead it, in order to soften it. As you knead, visualize the clay glowing with the energy of the deity, spirit, or principle you wish it to represent on your altar or shrine. Once it is soft, flatten it out with your hands.

4. Measure out the herbs into the dish. Hold the dish in your hands and say,

Herbs,
I call forth your qualities of protection,
peace, harmony, purification, abundance, and prosperity.
May my hearth always be blessed by these,
And may those who live in this house know good fortune,
health, and love.

5. Hold the dish of herbs in front of the candle so that the light of the flame shines on them. Say:

Sacred flame,
Bless these herbs.

6. Sprinkle the herbs evenly over the flattened clay. Roll the clay up, then form it into a ball. Knead it again to distribute the herbs throughout the clay.

7. Begin to form the clay into a rough shape approximating that of your idea for the figure. When you have the basic shape, begin smoothing it. Add details with tools such as a toothpick, a chopstick, or a skewer.

8. Leave the figure in a safe place to dry. If it has very thick areas, the clay may need more time to dry out properly. Turn it at some point so that it dries evenly.

9. When dry, you may paint your figure or leave it as it is. (Check the packaging of the clay for suggestions regarding what kind of paint to use.)

10. Place the figure on your shrine. Place a small dish of salt, rice, olive oil, or some other kind of offering. In your own words, thank the deity, spirit, or principle for its blessings, and ask that it remain always by your hearth, and bless your home.

Shrines Throughout the Home

The above suggestions regarding altars and shrines are equally applicable to any room in your house. If you are lucky enough to have a fireplace in your home, try using the mantelpiece as a shrine to the things you hold sacred. Photos of family, original artwork, candles, mirrors, colors and textures, statues or figurines all can be used to evoke a sense of your home, and of your connection with the sacred principles in your life as well as the Divine. Consider making it a family altar, with input from all members. Wherever the spiritual heart of your home is located, an altar or shrine can help confirm it and make it feel more real to you. All the above suggestions are easily applied or altered to create a shrine elsewhere in the home.

Shrines and altars don't need to be permanent, either. You can set one up for a specific event, or period in your life, or for a season. They can be set up anywhere in the home. Denise Linn's beautiful book *Altars: Bringing Sacred Shrines into Your Everyday Life* is an inspirational resource for this activity, as is Jean McMann's *Altars and Icons: Sacred*

Spaces in Everyday Life. Both are illustrated in full color and demonstrate the wide variety of ways in which people collect, arrange, and situate sacred displays that reflect and honor certain ideals, principles, milestones, or loved ones.

Being in the Moment: Acting Mindfully

If the kitchen is serving as the modern spiritual hearth, it stands to reason that any and all activity done in the room may qualify as having the potential for spiritual application. It's not as easy as declaring anything done within the kitchen as spiritual, however. While living one's life is a sacred undertaking, it's always hard to argue that taking out the trash qualifies as spiritual. The key is to be in a spiritual headspace while performing certain tasks.

If we argue that every moment has the potential to be spiritual, then what is required is a method of initializing that potential and making it real. Performing an action with awareness (also known as acting mindfully) offers this possibility.

Doing something with awareness is also known as being fully within the moment. Being in the moment means not thinking about what has happened previous to the present, or what you have to do next. It's granting the present task or situation your entire attention and focus and allowing it to unfold without forcing it or insisting that it occur in one way or another. Why is this considered a desirable thing? The main benefit of staying in the moment is that it engenders less stress. The position is relatively stress-free because there isn't an emphasis on "oh no I forgot to do something" or anxiety about what you have to do later, and therefore is more positive. This state is also more receptive to the healing and rejuvenating energy your spiritual hearth can provide. Being in the moment can help you appreciate the feel of your home and the impact your spiritual hearth has upon the people within it.

Perhaps the most important guiding principle for acting mindfully is to *perform one task at a time.* Multitasking is almost instinctive in today's world, but fight the drive to do as much as possible at once. You can't give your full attention to something if you're already dividing your attention between a number of tasks. This is one of my personal challenges; I find it very difficult to do one thing at a time. When I multitask, however, I tend to lose focus and not do a job as thoroughly as I would like, or I forget small parts of the task. If I "single-task" I somehow feel as if I'm not using my time efficiently. It's absolutely untrue, of course, but it's something I have difficulty shaking.

Being in the moment, however, offers me a way to engage my senses so that I feel as if I am extracting as much value from the situation as I possibly can. In her insightful book *French Women Don't Get Fat* Mireille Guiliano says of eating, "When you've learned to taste your food with care, you'll find yourself noticing the interplay of ingredients as never before." This is an excellent example of being in the moment: by allowing yourself to focus on a single task, you are allowing yourself to absorb as much information as possible about it and opening yourself to the spiritual energies involved, maximizing the potential for benefit.

Being in the moment sounds easy. If you've ever tried it, however, it isn't as simple as it sounds. Here are some suggestions to help you be in the moment:

- Be aware of your environment. What sounds do you hear? What is the light like? What are the smells around you? This helps anchor you in the real world that is around you right now.
- Be aware of yourself. How does your physical body feel? What are the textures of the clothes against your skin? How do you feel internally on a physical level? What is your emotional state? Do not judge any of these things; simply accept them for what they are.
- Imagine that you are seeing what is in front of you for the very first time. Come at it with new eyes. Don't simply accept what you see; observe it and allow yourself to absorb the details instead of assuming that you know what is there because you see it every day.
- Take at least three deep slow breaths. This is a commonly used technique to aid grounding, or reconnecting to the energy of the earth. It also features the bonus of delivering a good shot of oxygen to the lungs, which in turn oxygenates the blood.

It's impractical to consciously focus on every single move you make throughout the day as being spiritual. If we did we'd likely go slightly mad under all the perceived pressure and repercussions. It's generally enough to touch base with your spiritual hearth once a day and ask that your actions be blessed throughout the day.

We can mark certain actions or series of actions aside as consciously spiritual, however. Preparing a meal, for example, or tidying the kitchen make excellent examples of actions that can be consciously recognized as spiritual. It helps if you consciously assert this before each instance of the task. An excellent way to do this is to wash your hands. Water is considered a purifying element, apart from the basic physical association of cleaning with soap and water. Washing your hands with awareness makes an excellent trigger to signify the beginning of a spiritual act. It also provides a method of reconnecting to your spiritual hearth throughout the day, as it is a frequently performed action that can remind you to pause and reach out to engage with the power contained within your spiritual hearth, to restore or refresh yourself. Think of washing your hands as preparing yourself physically, emotionally, mentally, and spiritually for spiritual activity.

Here's an example of how to use washing your hands as a spiritual trigger.

1. Focus on being in the moment.
2. Turn the water on and let it run over your hands. Visualize the water washing away any negative or undesired energy.
3. Apply soap and wash your hands, keeping yourself in the moment. Notice how the soap feels on your skin, what the sensation of soapy skin over soapy skin feels like.
4. Rinse the soap off. Take three deep slow breaths, releasing any tension or stress you may be holding as you exhale.
5. Dry your hands with a clean cloth.

If you like, you can say a small prayer that you create yourself, or speak from the heart as you wash your hands.

By performing these steps with awareness and acknowledging that washing your hands is a spiritual act, you are signaling to your conscious and subconscious minds that you consider what you are about to do as important.

This is an excellent way to begin and end your day, as well. It provides you with an opportunity to be quiet and still for a moment, and to acknowledge the sanctity of the spiritual heart of your home. It is a moment of honoring it with respect, and honoring yourself as an integral element of that hearth. Doing it at the beginning of the day is a way to approach the day with openness and thanksgiving; doing it last thing at night before you turn off the kitchen light is a way to quietly thank your hearth.

Bringing Spirituality into Domestic Activity

Part of the trick to maintaining a home-based spiritual practice is to remind yourself frequently that your everyday life is a spiritual activity. The best way to do this is to establish a certain set of rituals to perform every day. By this I mean domestic activities that are set apart as ceremonial in some way, done with awareness and intent, not full-fledged ceremonial rituals in your kitchen. (Although if you want to do something like that, then go right ahead!) Regular tasks such as making coffee or setting the table are great tasks to which you can link a spiritual thought or act. It doesn't have to be complicated; it can be as basic as using the task to remind yourself that what you are doing is spiritual, just as everything else you do during the day and night is spiritual.

Here are some suggestions as to what you can do to add more spiritual awareness, support your spirituality and/or spiritual commitment during your kitchen-based activities.

+ **Meditation:** A lot of people sell meditation short, mainly because it's misunderstood or perceived as too difficult. Meditation can be as simple as sitting down in a tidied kitchen (or at least one free of crumbs, juice spills, and a stack of dishes in the sink) with a cup of tea, doing a series of body-relaxing exercises, and then just opening yourself up to the energy of the room and your home. You can choose something to think about, or just let your mind drift.

+ **Make offerings:** If you have a kitchen altar or shrine, touch base with it at least once a day. Offerings don't have to be big affairs; a pinch of an herb you're using to season a stew, a candle, even just a touch and a whispered "Thank you for being here" can do the trick.

+ **Make housework spiritual by recognizing the sacred in the tasks:** If you're washing the dishes or washing the floor, think about scrubbing the negativity away to reveal a pure and free object behind. Think of sweeping the kitchen like sweeping a temple: a clean place of worship or honoring is done out of respect for the deity or principle you're honoring.

+ **Prepare food with awareness:** Instead of throwing something together for a meal, take the time to be in the moment as you assemble it. There's more on this in Chapter 9.

+ **Consume food with awareness:** Some of us may associate saying grace before a meal with parental discipline, but it's a lovely idea. One such example is the Japanese Shinto practice of taking a moment before eating to thank the people who raised, harvested, transported, and were otherwise involved with getting the food from its natural state to your table. Even if it's a simple "Bless the hands who touched this food," a phrase like this spoken in quiet thanks provides you with a moment to reconnect with the world around you and the energy it emits.

+ **Wipe counters:** When you wipe counters down at night, think of clearing away all the clutter of thoughts and events that happened during the day, leaving both your hearth and your mind calm and balanced.

+ **Light a candle:** There is something very calming and spiritual about lighting a candle. It's a particularly fitting act for someone practicing hearthcraft, as the flame symbolizes so much about the practice. Try choosing a special candleholder and placing it on your kitchen shrine or somewhere particular in your kitchen, and lighting it before you begin work. Keep safety in mind when you choose where to place it: wax melts in heat, and many kitchen decorations and things like tea towels are flammable. As you light it, visualize or speak aloud a welcome to the essence of the flame and the blessing it bestows upon your hearth. If a candle isn't your thing or you want to try something different, see the following section on oil lamps.

Sacred Flame: Oil Lamps as Spiritual Tools

As the flame is one of the most common representations of the sacred, particularly in hearth-related spiritual paths, lighting a candle or some other kind of flame is a natural thing to do when you wish to have a physical representation of your spiritual hearth in the kitchen. As mentioned in Chapter 2, presence lamps are often employed by temples, churches, and shrines to signify the presence of the Divine.

Candles are lovely but require replacing on a frequent basis, and the heat of the kitchen as well as the drafts created by heat moving can make them burn unevenly or even damage the candle, depending on where you place it. Additionally, the open flame may make you nervous. A good solution to these problems is to use an oil-burning lamp, such as a hurricane lamp or some variation of it (also known as kerosene lamps or paraffin lamps). Lamps like this are fueled by liquid oil that is contained within the base. A wick of cloth or other fiber runs from the oil up through the neck of the lamp, and the flame burns at the tip of the wick. Fuel is constantly drawn up the wick through capillary action. Usually the flame of an oil lamp is protected by a glass chimney, allowing the light to be seen and cast out into the room but protecting the flame from drafts, and the height of the flame may be adjusted by turning a small screw that raises and lowers the wick, increasing or decreasing the amount of wick exposed above the fuel in the base.

There is another style of lamp that is sometimes referred to as an Aladdin lamp, but is more correctly called a *dipa*. A dipa (literally "lamp") is a Hindu oil lamp made from a roughly oval clay dish or bowl with one elongated end forming a small open spout-like channel, in which is laid a wick formed of twisted cotton that draws the oil in the bowl up to feed the flame burning at the other end of the wick at the edge of the spout. There is often a handle at the other end of the oval. Dipas in temples can be impressive brass candelabra-shaped affairs with these shallow dishes where candles would be placed, and a wick in each one, burning. Dipa-style lamps burning olive or other thick oils do not catch fire if tipped; the oil simply spreads and the flame dies.

The simplest kind of oil lamp can be made from any heat-safe dish and a wick from thin cotton string. Cut a piece of string about three inches long, and tie a knot in the middle of it. Trim the string until there is an inch on one side and approximately a half-inch on the other. Take a small piece of tin foil about a quarter-inch square, make a small hole in it with a thumbtack or pushpin, and thread the knotted string through it so that the knot rests on top. Bend the corners of the foil up slightly to make a dish shape. Float the square of foil on the top of the oil in the dish, knot side up. Wait a few minutes to allow the string to absorb oil, then light it. Trim this wick as necessary to avoid smoking and to obtain the best flame.

You can create a lamp out of any kind of container made from nonflammable material. Making your own lamp provides you with the opportunity to design it to reflect the spiritual goals you'll be using it for. Try making your own dish out of clay, shaping it into whatever style or shape you desire or feel inspired to mold. Dry it, glaze it to seal the inside surface, and fire it in a kiln. (Check your city's listings for ceramic groups or shops that can provide this service, or who can help you make the dish on site. Local schools may also offer evening workshops or classes.)

You can experiment with the following materials to find the perfect wick for your homemade lamp. In all cases, be certain that your material is one hundred percent cotton, and not blended with anything:

- Waxed candle wicks (make sure there's no metal wire inside)
- Spools of braided round or square wicking for candles
- Cotton batting, loosely twisted into a wick-like shape
- Cotton kitchen string

Make sure to use a saucer or dish under the lamp if you're using one that has a wick lying against the lip of the container; the capillary action that feeds the wick can leak oil over the edge.

Lighting an oil lamp when you work in the kitchen is a lovely way to signify that you are aware of the presence of the Divine. You can light this before each session in the kitchen, or first thing each morning. Safety indicates that you should extinguish it before you leave the house. As you do, say a prayer or something as simple as, "Although I extinguish the physical flame, the spiritual flame continues to burn both at the shrine and in my heart." Say this each time you extinguish the flame, and say something similar when you relight it when you return to the kitchen, such as, "I physically relight this sacred flame, reflecting the spiritual flame that burns continually at this shrine and in my heart."

When lighting it first thing in the morning, a more involved prayer is appropriate. Something along these lines, for example:

> *Sacred flame, symbol of purity and life,*
> *I light you now and invoke your sanctity.*
> *Descend upon the members of this household, and upon this room.*
> *Bless every person who enters it.*
> *Grant us peace, health, protection, and joy.*
> *I thank you for your many blessings, sacred flame.*

At the end of the day, extinguish the flame. This is associated with the traditional smooring of the hearth, the banking of the coals and embers to keep them alive but protected so that a fire could be easily built and lit the next morning (see Chapter 2). A prayer such as the following can be said:

> *Sacred flame, symbol of purity and life,*
> *I extinguish your physical form, although never your sanctity.*
> *We are grateful for your many blessings.*
> *Keep our family and home safe throughout the night.*
> *I thank you for your many blessings, sacred flame.*

The basic fuel used for oil lamps is kerosene, a clear thin water-like liquid with a slightly greasy feel to it. It is usually sold in two forms: kerosene and paraffin oil. Pure paraffin oil is a refined kerosene that burns with very little soot and odor, making it a good choice for indoor wick lamps. (It is not a liquid form of paraffin wax.) Always use the purest form of oil that you can afford or find to minimize airborne byproducts that may be hazardous to your health. Never use other fuels or oils that are not designated for use indoors, as the fumes created may be toxic. Avoid buying colored or scented lamp oils, as the fumes from the burning additives that lend the color and scent may not be as safe to breathe. Keep any oil lamp out of the reach of children, as well as the fuel.

> *In general, the thinner oils with a water-like consistency or viscosity work best in closed hurricane lamps, while thicker oils like olive and castor work better in dipa-style lamps.*

Using an oil lamp that burns olive oil is a particularly appropriate piece of equipment for this purpose, as opposed to an oil lamp that burns paraffin. Why use fossil fuel when you can burn a plant-based oil that is likely already in your kitchen? Additionally, the burning of the oil can be seen as an offering, which ties the oil lamp and the idea of offerings made to the spirits of the hearth nicely. Olive oil is of a thicker viscosity than kerosene, and the capillary action that draws the kerosene up the wick in a hurricane lamp is not strong enough to draw thicker oils to feed the flame. Therefore, if you are looking to use a thicker oil as a fuel for a presence flame, consider the dipa or dish-based style of lamp. Be vigilant about keeping the wick trimmed so that the oil does not gum up the wick and slow down or stop capillary action. Olive oil has been transported many miles and for that reason you may also object to it on an ethical basis for the transportation and fuel expended in bringing it to you. Other vegetable oils can be used as fuel for lamps as well with varying degrees of success and brightness of flame, such as coconut oil, castor oil, palm oil, and sweet almond oil. Clarified butter was used as a lamp oil in India, as Hindu culture holds the cow as sacred, and thus offerings of dairy products were often made.

The oil lamp provides you with a visible reminder of the spiritual hearth. Tending the lamp can be a satisfying act that engages you with physical activity while serving a spiritual function.

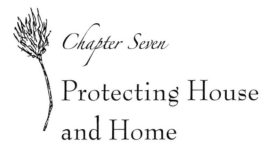

Chapter Seven

Protecting House and Home

One of the main foci of hearth magic revolves around protection, both of persons and possessions. This chapter focuses on how to maintain a clear and balanced energy within the home, how to cleanse and purify the atmosphere, how to handle threats, and how to build up magical defenses.

The home is the root of your family's energy and spirituality. If you are working to honor and strengthen it, and to make it as peaceful and spiritually nourishing as possible for you and your family, it only makes sense to protect it from harm or attack. Defending the repository of family power and source of family energy is like defending the supply wagons. Protection and purification are two of the most important concepts in home-based spirituality.

Basic Principles of Protecting House and Home

Common sense dictates that you defend your home physically by using secure locks, high fences with locking gates, security systems, locking windows, and so forth. Once this is done, however, there are many other things you can do to protect the home on a spiritual level.

Keeping track of your home's energy is important. The best way to do this is to be familiar with your home's regular energy, to be better able to identify shifts or changes, or problem areas that need to be dealt with. Being aware of your home's energy is crucial. Being familiar with its natural fluctuations, its cycles and responses to natural and environmental stimuli is an important factor in identifying and handling disruptions and problems.

Make a point of knowing every corner of your home, even (or perhaps especially) areas you don't frequent, such as storage areas, garage corners, the attic, and so forth. Don't forget the crawl space, if your home has one, or partial attics accessible through trapdoors or hatches in the ceiling of a closet somewhere. If you have a shed or outbuilding built onto the side or back of the house, get to know its energy as well. Physically walking through these areas allows you to touch their energies with your own, which in turn allows you a better sense of what they feel like, and also allows you to interact directly with the energy there.

An Overview of Your Home's Energy

This is an exercise that you can do to get a good overall sense of what your home's energy is like. Doing it yearly, or more frequently if your home is in a busy neighborhood, if you have a lot of people moving in and out, or a lot of emotional upheaval, is a good idea.

PREPARATION

Make a list of all the rooms and connecting spaces in and directly adjacent to your home. Physically walk through the house and make note of all these places. Doing the physical tour will help you see and remember all the little places you might otherwise forget. You might list the major rooms in your home off the top of your head—kitchen, living room, bedrooms, bathroom—but if you walk from one to another you may realize that you've forgotten the hallway, the stairs up to the second floor, the entryway between the front door and the hall, and the largish landing on the staircase that holds a table and a painting, among other places.

Don't forget storage cupboards, pantries, and linen closets either. All these spaces are separate, and serve separate functions. If you have an open-plan home or a large room that is separated into zones by function such as a family room that has a desk, a craft table for sewing, and a TV area, break the room down into those zones on your list (write down "family room: TV," "family room: sewing area" on your list). It's important to understand the function each room in your house serves because it affects the energy produced and held within the room. A mismatch between the room's envisioned function and the purpose it actually serves can create a skewed energy too; exploring this can help you refocus the energy in your rooms and remove what negatively affects the desired energy.

Make a chart like the following:

1. Room name:
   _____

2. Date:
   _____

3. Adjacent rooms:
   _____

4. Cardinal position:
   _____

5. Use:
   _____

6. Energy observations:
   _____

7. Suggestions or recommendations:
   _____

8. Miscellaneous:
   _____

When you've got your list, pick a room and go back to it. Go through the chart item by item and make your notes.

ROOM NAME AND DATE

This sounds obvious, but you're going to be keeping these notes to refer back to and while things may seem fresh in your mind now, I guarantee that after you've done this you won't necessarily remember when you did it. After the date, write down the weather, moon phase, day of the week, time of day, or any other associated information that you think interesting or that you believe may affect the energy readings you will take. This is as much of a way to evaluate how you interact with your home's energy as it is an assessment of the house energy itself.

It can be revelatory later to go through these papers and realize that you can't do a clear energy evaluation when the moon is full, for example.

ADJACENT ROOMS AND CARDINAL POSITION

When you note this down, don't forget to include what rooms are above and below the room you are in. The energy of these rooms impacts the room's energy as well. The cardinal position helps further situate the location. Does the room face west, or north-east? This can be important if there is something such as a large shopping mall or a body of water in one direction or another. These things have large fields of energy that can affect your home as well, and often have a greater effect on the rooms closer to them. When you're done, look at what rooms adjoin one another, and see what kinds of energy are interacting through the wall or floor. If you live in an apartment, chances are good your next-door neighbor isn't going to allow you into his or her home to "sense the energy" of the room adjoining your wall. Apartments are a different kettle of fish. Assume the energy on the other side is on the bad side of neutral, and create wards and shields accordingly. Better to be safe than sorry.

USE

What is this room used for? Rooms have an interesting habit of adapting to a family's needs, and the original use of the room is often modified as the family's needs change. First, list what it is supposed to be used for (library? den? office? playroom?). Then, list what actually happens in the room (video games? TV watching? ironing? homework?). Sometimes the energy in a room is more conducive to something else rather than what you slated it to be when you moved in.

ENERGY OBSERVATIONS

How does the room feel to you? If you walk into the middle of it and close your eyes, how does it affect you emotionally? Do you feel relaxed? Tense? Angry? Sleepy? Now open your eyes and sense how it feels to you with the added visual information. Note both down. Walk through the room and see if your feelings change from location to location. Within the overall energy of a room there are very often several pockets of energy stronger in one sense than another. Draw a rough map of these energy sensings.

SUGGESTIONS OR RECOMMENDATIONS

These can be spiritual, magical, or physical in nature. Should you move the furniture around? Remove a piece? Add a piece? Change the color scheme? Switch the room with another to make better use of the energies in each location? Should you add a certain elemental energy to balance an excess or lack of a certain element? Is an immediate purification indicated to cleanse the energy of something negative?

MISCELLANEOUS

This is a place to write down something that doesn't fit somewhere else. Is there something in the room that needs repair? A reminder you want to set for yourself?

Look back over your notes. You should have what is in essence a snapshot of your home's energy as it stands at the present moment. This reference can be used as a baseline when you sense something odd or different in your home.

Boundaries and Thresholds

Setting up energy barriers or boundaries is a good way to not only keep track of what is happening with your home's energy at all times, but to control what kind of energy comes into it. The threshold is a logical place to encode with a spiritual barrier. As the natural entrance and egress to your home, it can serve as a filter or blockade for undesired energy. Windows also should be protected, as they make easy alternatives to doors.

The threshold is a magical place, as it is neither in the house nor out, and yet it is part of both. Using the threshold as a focus for a protective spell is a first defense.

Threshold Protection Ritual

This ritual not only cleanses the threshold, but empowers it to function as a filter to allow positive energy into the home while keeping negative or disruptive energy out.

This creates a protective barrier keyed to the threshold of your house. If you have more than one entrance you use regularly, perform this ritual at the entrance you use more frequently, then at the secondary entrance.

You will need:

+ 1 cup of water
+ ½ cup of vinegar
+ 1 tablespoon of salt
+ 1 tablespoon of lemon juice

- bowl or bucket
- washing cloth
- sage smudge (or loose dried sage, a charcoal tablet, and a censer)
- matches or lighter
- sealing oil (see Chapter 11, or use a tablespoon of olive oil with a pinch of salt added to it)
- 3 cloves of garlic

1. Blend the water, vinegar, salt, and lemon juice together in a bowl or bucket. With the cloth, use this mixture to wash the threshold and doorframe. Be thorough: scrub the threshold inside and out, as well as the doorframe on both sides of the door, and both sides of the door itself.

2. Light the sage smudge and move it around the doorframe, wafting the smoke so that it touches the area inside and out. Lay the smudge in a censer or heatproof dish and allow it to smolder while you complete the ritual.

3. Dip your finger in the sealing oil and draw an unbroken line around the outside of the doorframe. Dip your finger in the oil again as necessary, but begin again exactly where you left off, or retrace an inch or so of the line to ensure its continuity. As you draw the line, say:

No evil or illness may cross this threshold.
I hereby bar it from entering.
My home is sacred, and protected.

4. Dip your finger in the oil again. On the inside of the doorframe, touch your finger to the upper left corner, and trace a line in the air down and across the doorway to touch the lower right corner. Dip your finger in the oil again, touch it to the upper right corner, and draw a line in the air down and across to touch the lower left corner. Dip your finger one last time and touch it to the middle of the lintel above the door, and draw a line in the air straight down to touch the middle of the threshold. As you do, say again:

No evil or illness may cross this threshold.
I hereby bar it from entering.
My home is sacred, and protected.

This symbol is a hexefus, or a combination of the runes Isa (a vertical line) and Gebo (an X). Gebo represents exchanges of energy or material objects, while Isa represents a static state (it translates to "ice"). Drawn together in this bindrune form, Isa "freezes" the state of your home and possessions, protecting it from both physical and other intrusion.

5. Take three cloves of garlic. Touch each of them with a finger dipped in the oil. Bury them under your threshold or doorstep, or as near to it as possible. Bury one at each end of the step or threshold, and one in the middle. As you do, say again one final time:

No evil or illness may cross this threshold.
I hereby bar it from entering.
My home is sacred, and protected.

If you like, you can adapt this ritual and apply it to your windows as well. Bury a single clove of garlic in the ground under each window.

Wards

A ward is something that protects or defends. When used in connection with a house or home, generally, to ward something is to set up an autonomous system of protection.

The caveat is that you have to check on it regularly. Just like raising a wall around a city to defend it, if you don't take a regular walk around and look at the state of the wall you've built, it can crumble, grow weak, be affected by the weather or vines. You can't just raise it and ignore it; it needs to be refreshed now and again. How often depends on the kind of neighborhood you live in.

This is a good basic ward for your home. It needs frequent renewal. Two or four times a year is good; try tying it to the seasonal shifts. If you feel the ward has been compromised in some way, take it down (see below) and reconstruct it afresh.

You will need:

+ a candle in a candleholder
+ a dish of water
+ a dish of earth (you may use salt, but as you will be sprinkling this on the ground it's not advisable)
+ incense (your choice)
+ censer
+ matches or lighter

1. Light the candle. Beginning at your threshold, walk around the outside of your dwelling, carrying the candle in front of you. As you walk, say:

I build this boundary with fire.

Repeat the sentence as you walk all the way around the building. Visualize the path the flame traces hanging in the air as a band of energy. When you return to your threshold, set down the candle.

2. Pick up the dish of water and walk around the building again, dipping your fingers into the water and sprinkling it as you walk. As you do, say:

I build this boundary with water.

Repeat the sentence as you walk all the way around the building. Visualize the path the water traces hanging in the air as a band of energy. When you return to your threshold, set down the dish of water.

3. Pick up the dish of earth and walk around the building again, dipping your fingers into the earth and sprinkling it as you walk. As you do, say:

I build this boundary with earth.

Repeat the sentence as you walk all the way around the building. Visualize the path the earth traces hanging in the air as a band of energy. When you return to your threshold, set down the dish of earth.

4. Light the incense and place it in the censer. Pick it up and walk around the building again, wafting the smoke around you as you walk. As you do, say:

I build this boundary with air.

Repeat the sentence as you walk all the way around the building. Visualize the path the smoke traces hanging in the air as a band of energy. When you return to your threshold, set down the censer.

5. Standing at your threshold, reach out with your hands as if you were placing your palms on a wall. Visualize the four circuits you made with the elements fusing together, expanding into a solid wall of energy. Then visualize that wall of energy growing down into the ground and curving in until it meets under your dwelling. Visualize the top growing up and in until it meets overhead, thus forming a sphere of energy enclosing the building. Say:

Fire, water, earth, and air,
Guard this home against all ill will and danger.
Keep this house and those who live in it safe.
I declare this ward to be raised and active.

Removing a Ward

A word of advice about wards and protective barriers: If you're keeping something out, you're also keeping something in at the same time. It's healthy to lower wards and barriers now and again to allow what you've trapped inside to move around and air the place out, so to speak.

Sometimes a ward must be dismantled. If you move, for example, or if your home energy alters significantly in some way (the addition of a new member of the family or lodger, for example, or a major change in career, or a physical alteration of the house through renovation or addition) the original ward, programmed to recognize and protect a certain energy and home entity, can become less effective. Dissolving it or taking it down is a smart step before rebuilding a new ward. Rather than try to reshape and adapt what you originally put up, release the energy of the ward and start afresh. Building on the old ward is inadvisable because it has its foundations in something that technically no longer exists.

To dissolve an existing ward, begin at your threshold and walk counter-clockwise around your dwelling. As you do, hold your hand out with the palm down and visualize it slicing through the wall or boundary you constructed when you raised the ward. As you walk, say:

> *I dissolve this ward.*
> *You have my thanks for your protection in the past.*
> *I release you with my blessing.*

When you return to your threshold stamp your foot on it to shake loose the ties to any remaining energy of the past ward and say,

I declare this ward dissolved.

Other Protective Techniques

Folk magic and cultural customs are a treasure-trove of protective techniques. Here are some I've encountered:

✦ Paint magical symbols on walls/ceilings for a specific purpose, using salt water, or lemon water.

✦ If you get the chance to do it before you repaint a room, do it in the same color of paint before you paint over it. This will be permanent; think well.

✦ Walk your property boundaries with cornmeal and water (separately), asking blessings and friendship of the spirits of the land, to guard and protect those who live here.

✦ Salt water left out in the center of a room all night will absorb negativity. Wash it away with flowing water the next morning.

✦ Placing a mirror in a window on each side of your home, facing outwards, will reflect negativity back to the sender. Likewise hanging a witch ball, a polished glass globe, in the window will absorb and return negative energy.

✦ Bells or wind chimes hung from the doors guard against intruders and stagnant energy. Hang them where the air currents can ring them. They will set up movement in the air and clear the psychic energy of your home.

- Hang a mirror empowered to reflect negative energy inside, facing the front door.
- Bury protective stones such as onyx, malachite, or amethyst under your doorstep, porch, or steps.
- Wash your doorstep with purifying wash (see Chapter 11).
- Hang Pennsylvania Dutch hex signs associated with protection inside and outside your house.
- Hang an iron horseshoe above your door, with the open end facing upward.

Using Stones

Stones and gems are frequently used as protective objects for their associated energies and qualities. These stones in particular are good to use in the home:

- **Amethyst:** absorbs negative energy, promotes harmony
- **Amber:** health, prevents energy drain, transforms negative energy to positive energy
- **Apache tear:** encourages harmony in times of stress
- **Aventurine:** defends prosperity and health
- **Carnelian:** success, creativity, protection from nightmares, equalizes emotions such as anger and grief
- **Hematite:** reflects negativity
- **Jade:** wisdom, fidelity
- **Lapis lazuli:** harmony, serenity
- **Malachite:** prosperity, abundance, protection
- **Obsidian:** absorbs negative energy
- **Onyx:** happiness, good luck

- **Quartz crystal:** transforms negative energy to positive, source of energy for those in the home
- **Rose quartz:** transforms negative energy into positive energy, encourages affection
- **Tiger eye:** stability, wealth

Trees and Plants

One of the easiest things to do to protect your house is to plant trees, shrubs, and plants associated with defense and protection around it. If you're thinking of planting a tree on your property, you can choose one that has protective associations, thereby extending the tree's value to your home and land as well. If you already have one of these trees on your land or near your home, introduce yourself to it and thank it for the energy it emanates.

- **Hawthorn:** protects against damage from storms, encourages happiness
- **Birch:** protects children
- **Rowan:** protects health
- **Hazel:** protects against evil; encourages abundance and inspiration
- **Oak:** defends against physical harm
- **Sassafras:** defends from evil spirits
- **Elder:** defends against evil and negative energy
- **Lilac:** defends against harmful spirits

When you plant a tree for protection, you can say a prayer such as the following:

Sacred tree [or bush],
Grant us your protection.
May your roots defend us against harm from below,
May your branches defend us against harm from above.
May your leaves and shade
Extend your protection to our home and property.
In return we will care for you, sacred tree,
And guard you against blight and drought.
Sacred tree, we welcome you to our family.

If you don't own land but there is an existing tree nearby that you wish to use as part of your house and home protection, introduce yourself to it by spending time sitting with it. Get to know its energy and decide if you wish to incorporate it into your work. Trees, like other natural objects, are living creatures and may or may not feel open to working with you. After getting to know its energy over a few days, offer the tree water, and ask it if it is willing to work with you as a home guardian. Trust your intuition for the answer.

Purifying and Cleansing the Home

For anyone in tune with the energies of the home, purifying and cleansing is an essential element of their practice. To maintain the home's balanced energy, establish a set number of times throughout the year to do cleansings, purifications, and blessings. They don't all have to be major undertakings: like physical housework, the more often you do it, the lighter the workload is each time.

You may choose to vary the schedule. For example, you may do a deep, major purification twice a year (on the solstices, perhaps), with minor purifications on the first day of each month, or at each full or dark moon. Or you may choose to do a regular mid-level cleansing and blessing on each sabbat or bank holiday. Choose a time that will work for you and blend into your schedule with the least amount of awkwardness. If you prefer your spiritual or energy work to be associated with moon phases or holy days, schedule your house purifications around those times. Then decide if you will do it before the date in order to have your house cleansed and ready to experience the energy of the day in question, or if you will do your work on the day itself to take advantage of the associated energy for your purification, or do the work directly following the day in order to have a clean slate for the energies of the next section of the cycle. Alternately, perhaps you function best on a regular calendar-type schedule, and planning a regular purification on the same date every month will help you keep the rhythm.

There is no right or wrong way. Do what makes sense to you, and what feels right. The point is to do it regularly, as regularly as your space requires and your schedule allows.

The frequency of purification and cleansing depends on the energy of your home, which is one of the reasons the above exercise is indicated. If your home sees heavy traffic from visitors or heavy emotional situations, it may be best to purify more often than if you live alone.

Purification Techniques

There are dozens of ways to purify a room of unwanted energy. Before we go on, let's take a moment to talk about negative energy versus unwanted energy. Negative energy is also unwanted; we generally strive for as positive an environment as possible in the home. However, there are also energies that can be classified as neutral through positive that for some reason may not be suitable for the atmosphere you are seeking to create in a specific space. For this reason, the term "banishing" isn't used here. Banishing something creates a vacuum of sorts, an empty space that must and will be filled with something else. If you consciously banish something then logic dictates that you should be prepared to consciously replace it with positive energy. But banishing neutral through positive energy doesn't make sense, and for that reason the term transform or reprogram is more appropriate.

If the negative energy is occupying a space that has a natural positive vibration to it, then absorbing or removing the negative energy will generally result in the return of the natural positive balance.

Some of the following techniques are more active than others. For example, smudging with chosen herbs is a more active process than leaving a sliced onion in a room to absorb unwanted energy.

While at heart most of these techniques address the removal of negative energy, most can be consciously programmed to affect other energies as well.

Sage and Herb Smudging

Many cultures employ a technique of purifying via smoke created by burning plant matter considered sacred or honored in some way. Incense is one such example. Smudging with sage is a Native American technique that has proven very adaptable and effective for people of any tradition and spiritual path. Essentially, a bundle of dried herbs is lit and the flame extinguished, leaving the dry plant matter to smolder and produce a smoke that has the qualities of the plant matter itself. This smoke is easily wafted around a room or other space, can insinuate into nooks and crannies, and has the ability to surround objects. It is also less likely to damage objects, whereas water or flame (two of the other popularly recognized purifiers) can damage things. The bundle of herbs is referred to as a smudge or a smudge stick, and is easily carried in the hand. The act of surrounding someone or something with the smoke is called smudging. Smudging may also be done by crumbling dried plant matter on a charcoal tablet.

Sage is the original and most popular herb to use in this respect, but there are other popular herbs commonly used such as cedar, sweetgrass, and lavender. These four herbs generally encourage a calm atmosphere with positive energy. Sage and cedar in particular are considered sacred herbs in the Native American traditions.

There's no right or wrong way to make a smudge stick, but here's a general guideline. To make a smudge, lay several dried stalks of your chosen herb(s) together. Slip a length of natural undyed cotton string under one end of the bundle and begin wrapping the stalks, crisscrossing the string over and under the bundle, tying it at various intervals. Wrap it firmly but not so tightly that the stalks are completely crushed together; air needs to circulate through the bundle in order to maintain the smoldering process. Tie the ends of the string firmly at the other end of the bundle. Wrapping and tying the smudge in this way allows the bundle to stay tied when you begin burning it and the string at the end burns through. Don't worry if bits of the dried herb break off as you wrap the smudge.

Stalks that are too thick will not burn well; stalks that are too thin will snap when you wrap the bundle. Don't make a bundle that is more than an inch and a half in diameter once it's wrapped and tied; it will be difficult to keep smoldering. A smudge smaller than a half-inch may be too fragile. If you prefer, you may harvest your own fresh herbs and wrap them while fresh, then hang the bundle up in a well-ventilated place to dry thoroughly. The bundle must be completely dry before using it, or it will not burn properly. Watch it carefully during the drying process, to ensure that the bundle does not grow mildew.

When you smudge, do so with respect for the act, awareness, sensitivity, and while visualizing your goal. You may say a short prayer or invocation before beginning or not, as you feel necessary. Something as simple as "Sage (or whatever single or combination of herbs you are using), I call upon your sacred energy to cleanse this space" can work. Light one end of the smudge by touching it to a flame, and make sure the smudge has caught well before gently blowing the flame out. The ends of the dry herbs should still glow red and give off smoke. Air needs to move through the smudge to keep it smoldering, and you can do this by fanning it gently with your free hand. This movement also allows you to direct the smoke into corners and around objects. You may also use a feather. If you carry the smudge around the room in your hand, bits of burning plant matter will fall onto the floor. Smudges are often laid in a heatproof container such as a shell, earthenware bowl (unglazed ceramic or clay works well), or a rock with a depression in it, to catch these bits.

The entire smudge need not be used. You can extinguish it in a bowl of salt or sand, making extremely certain that it has completely gone out, and wrap it in aluminum foil or store it in a paper bag until your next smudging.

Smudging may also be used to purify an object before use, or to clear accumulated energy from a tool.

Burning Incense

Like smudging, burning incense releases smoke that carries the energy of the incense's ingredients. The point of this is to get that energy moving around in an easily dispersible way. You could sprinkle the actual herbs around, but gravity will probably make it difficult to access higher pockets of the energy you're trying to move.

You can use preprepared incense from a retailer in a scent or formula specifically prepared for purification, or a pure scent that is associated with purification. Cedar, sage, lavender, and frankincense are single scents that are often used to purify; blends labeled "Purification" often include these. Preprepared incense usually comes in stick or cone form.

Stick incense can be made in one of two ways: rolled (which is made from a wet mixture of ingredients then rolled into a thin cylinder and dried, sometimes around a thin stick to give it support), and dipped (a blank stick with a neutral paste molded around it, which is then dipped into a solution of oils). Cone incense, like rolled incense, is made from a paste of ingredients, then shaped. Sticks and cones are usually self-combustible, meaning they do not require a charcoal tablet to burn them. By lighting the end of a stick or cone, waiting until the tip glows red, then gently blowing out the flame, the incense will burn on its own. Sticks and cones are convenient and do not require anything other than a bowl with salt or sand in which to burn them and catch the ashes, although censers (also known as incense burners) are easy to find. Censers for sticks are usually long curved flat pieces of stone or wood, with tiny holes at one end into which the sticks are inserted, which hold the stick at an angle so the ash falls onto the burner.

Loose incense is literally that: a blend of roughly ground or chopped plant matter that must be burned on a charcoal tablet in order to release its energy in the form of smoke. This is my favorite kind of incense, as it is the easiest kind to make at home, and can be made in almost any proportion mostly from ingredients in your pantry or spice cabinet.

Here are some commonly found kitchen herbs that you can use in a purifying incense:

- Cinnamon
- Clove
- Rosemary
- Sage
- Thyme

Things you can find in your garden, dry, and then add:

- Lavender
- Rose

And finally, resins are an ingredient you'll have to purchase, but they can really make your incense extra special:

- ✦ Frankincense
- ✦ Benzoin
- ✦ Golden copal

Alternatively, you can use the essential oil of any of these ingredients, and add a couple of drops to the dry ingredients, and mix it all together well.

To test the incense, you'll need a charcoal tablet and a bowl filled with salt or sand in which to burn it. Light the charcoal tablet by holding the edge of it to a flame. (Be careful; it can ignite quickly. You may want to use tweezers or small tongs to hold it safely.) When the charcoal begins to spark, put it down in the salt- or sand-filled bowl. When the sparks have finished traveling across the surface of the tablet and the charcoal begins to glow red in patches, it is ready. Take a pinch of your incense and place it on the charcoal. Observe how it reacts so that you'll be prepared for it when you first use it in a larger quantity. Don't put more than a teaspoon of loose incense on the charcoal tablet at a time, or you may smother the charcoal as well as have to open a window to clear some of the smoke! It's a good idea to have an extra bowl of sand to dump on top of the charcoal tablet if you need to extinguish it quickly. Be careful; sometimes charcoal will continue to smolder. To make sure it's really out, pour water over it.

Burning dry herbs never smells like the essential oil or the dry herb itself in a bottle. In fact, it can be smell pretty much like burning leaves or grass, which isn't always pleasant. To offset the burning-leaf smell you can add resins, as resins tend to have a sweeter smell than dried plant matter does.

Purifying Incense

Blending your own purifying incense means you're using exactly the kind of energies you want to use in your house. And when you do it with clear intent and awareness, you're adding an extra dimension of personal energy to the process, keying it to your home and family and spiritual practice. Here's a basic recipe for loose purifying incense.

You will need:

+ 1 teaspoon frankincense resin
+ 1 teaspoon copal resin
+ ½ teaspoon dried lavender
+ ½ teaspoon rosemary
+ pinch of ground cloves
+ mortar and pestle
+ small bottle or jar with lid

1. Place the frankincense and copal resin in the mortar. Gently crush the resin with the pestle. Transfer it to the jar. If there is any residue left in the mortar, scrape it out gently and add it to the jar. Resin tends to melt under enthusiastic grinding, and can gum up the mortar. Be gentle, and don't feel that you have to reduce the fragments to powder. Chips that are smaller than the granules the resin arrived in is fine.
2. Place the lavender and rosemary in the mortar. Grind them into smaller pieces, and transfer to the jar.
3. Add the pinch of ground clove to the jar.
4. Cap the jar and gently shake it to combine all the ingredients.

Folk Techniques for Purifying

Tradition and folklore provides us with dozens of ways to clear bad luck, negative energy, bad feelings, and unwanted nasties from rooms and other places. Common and popular purification techniques include:

+ Burning candles
+ A slice of onion left on a saucer in the center of the room to absorb negative energy
+ A slice of lemon left on a saucer in the center of the room to absorb negative energy
+ A bowl of water left to absorb unwanted energy
+ Stones programmed to absorb unwanted energy
+ Asperging with salt water
+ Asperging with herbal water (herbs left to soak in water for a specific time, drained, then dispersed via herb bundle or spray bottle)
+ Sprinkling salt around a room (and vacuuming it up later)
+ Sprinkling powdered or ground herbs around a room (and vacuuming it up later)
+ Dispersing essential oil into the air via an aromatherapy jar
+ Hanging strings of garlic or onions in the kitchen to absorb negative energy

Note that in some places energy is referred to as *unwanted*, not negative. There are times when an energy is positive, but not wanted in a specific place. For example, energy that soothes and promotes sleep is a positive kind of energy, but not desirable in a home office where you want to be alert and productive. Of course, the unwanted energy may be negative as well.

You may find that certain rooms respond better to specific techniques. That's fine. Use the technique that works best in the room you're purifying. It may be a bit more work to switch techniques if you're doing a full house purification, but in the long run it's best for the overall energy of the home. The point is to be as effective and efficient as possible, and while changing techniques may use a bit more time, it promotes a smoother household, which in turn affects everything done inside it.

Terms such as purify, cleanse, and bless are often used interchangeably, but they do mean slightly different things.

- *To cleanse something means to remove the physical dirt from it, with the intent to remove any associated energy influence.*
- *To purify something means to remove the negative or undesired energy from it.*
- *To bless something means to infuse the item with positive Divine-influenced or -originated energy.*

If you plan to purify a space for the first time, or for the first time in a long time, do all three of them in order. Begin by cleansing the room, then purify it, and finally ask Spirit or your concept of the Divine or your spiritual hearth to bless it. For the less intense maintenance rituals, you may choose to do the purification alone. For a touch of spiritual energy as the mood or desire strikes you, the blessing is ideal.

Basic Room Purification Ritual

This is an all-purpose purification ritual that can be used as is or as a basis for your own ritual.

You will need:

+ Cleaning supplies (as required)
+ Incense (stick or loose)
+ Censer or heatproof bowl
+ Salt or sand (if using bowl for incense)
+ Charcoal tablet (if using loose incense)
+ Candle (white or color of your choice)
+ Candleholder
+ Matches or lighter

1. Begin by physically cleaning the space. Tidy the room. Put things in their place, or return them to their original places in other rooms. Then vacuum, sweep, dust, polish—do whatever you need to do to remove physical dirt. It can be as thorough as you feel it needs to be.
2. Purify the room by burning a teaspoonful of your favorite purifying incense (or use the recipe on p. 140) on a charcoal tablet. Alternatively, use a stick of purchased incense in a purifying scent, or use a smudge stick (homemade or purchased). As you light it say:

I light this incense to purify this space.

3. Place the bowl or censer in the middle of the room, and let the smoke fill the space. More incense is not necessarily better; a single small spoonful can produce billows of smoke depending on the blend you're using. Make sure you test the blend beforehand. If you like, you can walk around the room in a counterclockwise direction to help disperse the smoke throughout the space. Counter-clockwise movement is associated with banishing or undoing something.

4. Allow the incense to purify the room for as long as you feel it is necessary. It may take anywhere between a few minutes to a few hours. Don't worry about keeping the incense burning all that time; let the energies released with the original spoonful or stick do their work. If you sense that it will take longer than the initial burn time, check on the room or space after an hour (or after the incense has finished burning, or once the smoke has cleared) to evaluate to see if you need to burn more incense, or follow up with another purifying technique.

5. When the space feels purified, light the candle and place it in the middle of the space, saying:

I light this flame to bless this space.

Allow it to burn down.

Regular Maintenance

Regular housecleaning has a magical function as well. If you're a reluctant housecleaner (and most of us are; dusting, mopping, and vacuuming are rarely high on the list of Fun Things to Do) thinking of chores as the opportunity to do some spiritual housecleaning can make the difference between doing the chore grudgingly and doing it willingly. Remember that your energy, your emotional state, and your frame of mind color the energy of your actions so if you're doing something grudgingly the energy that comes from your grumpy resistance is going to influence and affect the outcome. If you're cleaning, the last thing you want is unwilling or sulky energy to attach itself to what you're cleaning.

This means you may need to set the stage for yourself and create the right ambiance, so to speak. Make it an enjoyable experience, as best you can. If you have trouble finding time to express yourself spiritually, or are looking for another opportunity to connect with the spiritual part of your life and spirit, why not use this time? The repetitive movement of sweeping or wiping a window can be meditative.

Clean and Tidy

It's said that the best defense is a good offense, and it's certainly true in the case of order and cleanliness. Keeping order in your home is a way of keeping in touch with the energies that flow through it.

The term "order" suggests a specific arrangement, not just tidy, and this is an essential part of keeping your home a harmonious place. "A place for everything and everything in its place" is an axiom that has merit. If your home is a sea of clutter, the energy will be equally chaotic. I'm not advocating a magazine-perfect house; those always strike me as impossible to actually *live* in. By order I mean a proper organizing of objects and items. Things tend to migrate in houses, thanks to the people using them. It's important that things be returned to their correct places. If everything was allowed to stay where it was left, certain parts of the home would rapidly become unusable. A chaotic jumble of toys and books and clothes and general stuff creates an equally chaotic energy, which in turn can sabotage the harmonious atmosphere you're striving to create and maintain.

Let me stress that a lot of possessions in a smallish space does not necessarily equate to chaos. You may be one of those people who pulls together a home of bric-a-brac and wall ornaments and decoration, and that energy is part of what makes your home yours: the energy created by how all those things interact is part of your home and hearth's identity. But if you do have a lot of stuff, making sure it's kept organized is even more important. Your home doesn't have to look like those in the pages of home magazines—most of us wouldn't really like to live there anyway—but it should show a coherent order of some kind. And realize that your coherent order isn't necessarily someone else's. If your order succeeds, people will feel comfortable in your home even if it isn't their style.

The kind of energy created by the interaction of your furniture and possessions can be changed or otherwise affected by rearranging it or otherwise altering the contents of a room. Things possess energies of their own to different degrees, and together they create a larger collective energy. Adding things to the collective energy, or taking them away, can influence the feel of a room.

The flow of energy within a room is important. Often a room is unwelcoming because the energy within it doesn't flow; instead, it is stagnant. If you don't sense how this happens (either by deliberate energy sensing or a vague feeling concerning the room), try standing in the doorway to the room and looking in. Where are your eyes drawn right away? What path do they trace if you don't deliberately turn them in one direction or another? Chances are good that's the path the energy of the room takes too. If your eyes don't naturally move around the room, chances are good the energy doesn't either. If there's an area that is unused, despite having chairs or other furniture and equipment provided, the flow of energy through the room may not reach there, or it may be blocked by something.

To attract or encourage certain kinds of energy, place objects or symbols associated with that energy in key areas. This can be a major rearrangement, or something unobtrusive. You can place small images that carry or represent desired energy in corners or nooks and crannies: a small image of a bee in a "dead" corner, for example, can help keep it vibrant, for the bee is a symbol of activity, community, and industry.

Don't overlook the smell of a room, either. We tend to get used to the particular blend of odors our homes possess, but you have probably walked into someone else's house and been struck immediately by the scent of it. Sometimes it isn't an appealing scent, either. Staleness or damp smells can be overlooked in our own home because we're used to the particular blend of aromas. The scent of a home is part of its identity, however, and affects the energy just as visual presentation does. Keeping corners and windowsills clean can inhibit the accumulation of odor-causing mold, while sprinkling baking soda on sofas and carpets and leaving it for a few hours to absorb odors before vacuuming it away can help refresh the smell of a room. Opening windows to air out a room is another simple remedy that can refresh the air and energy in your home.

Chapter Eight
Magic in the Kitchen

In the context of hearthcraft, magic may be seen as a way of consciously drawing on the energy of the spiritual hearth to enhance the activity in which you are engaging. In essence, magic describes the conscious action of bringing together different energies and directing them toward a positive spiritual goal. In many paths magic and spiritual practice are separate, but in hearthcraft the magical activity both supports and draws from spiritual activity. As so much of hearthcraft revolves around love, nurturing, and protection of what we consider sacred, positive goals can be the only ones envisioned.

Another way of looking at magic within the context of hearthcraft is as transformation of some kind, a task performed with the intent to weave together energies in order to initiate some sort of spiritual transformation, rejuvenation, or growth.

With that in mind, then, this chapter looks at kitchen folklore and customs, and at the energies associated with the equipment found and used in the kitchen. We know that everything possesses energy to some extent, and that symbols also carry specific energies. (If you're interested in exploring this further, you may read *Power Spellcraft for Life* or *The Way of the Green Witch* for more information and exercises designed to explore energy and techniques for sensing and working with it.) The section on tools in the latter half of this chapter looks at the equipment found in modern kitchens and poses a few questions about their energy and how it affects and supports the energy of your spiritual hearth.

Hearth and Home Journal

If you've read any of my other books you know how insistent I am about keeping records. Keeping track of what you did when helps you plan and schedule your activity, as well as offering you the opportunity to review your past activity for insight. At its most basic, a journal can be a collection of ideas and notes about what goes right and wrong, or a place to store the tidbits of home-related information you collect about spirituality or everyday life.

Your journal is the place to copy recipes, rituals, ceremonies, purifications, and any other specific spiritual activity you do. You can be as specific as you like, including notes about the weather, who else was in the house at the time, your impression and emotional state, and so forth. It's a place to record bits of information about deities or spirits that you research, the meditations you do, the offerings you make and how you feel they were received. You can make diary entries about how you feel, the connections you make, and your thoughts about your practice of home-based spirituality. You can paste in color swatches, clippings from magazines, or paint chips if you're planning to redecorate, and insert photographs of your house at different stages to record its evolution through the years. You can keep track of the dinner parties you host, writing down the menu, the guests invited, and the culinary successes (or failures!). You can press flowers or leaves from your garden in it. You can record poems or prayers in it. In short, it's a catch-all for anything associated with your spiritual path, for ease of later reference.

You can use a blank notebook with lined or unlined pages, or a three-ring binder. The binder allows your inserted pages to expand as necessary, whereas the bound notebook may soon no longer close properly. It works best to use something that is at least 8 by 10 inches, to allow yourself room to record and draw and paste things in.

The Magic of Materials

The materials we work with all possess their own energies. Here's a look at the common materials found in the kitchen, and their associated magical energies to help you get a handle on what they contribute to the energy of your home. Being aware of these energies means you can actively incorporate them into your spiritual work and take advantage of their benefits.

There were seven main metals known to the ancients. Each was associated with a planet (which in turn had already been associated with a deity) and assigned a sympathetic set of associations and correspondences. The seven metals of the ancients were gold (associated with the sun), silver (the moon), quicksilver (Mercury), copper (Venus), iron (Mars), tin (Jupiter), and lead (Saturn). Many of these metals are still used in today's homes, and are listed below with their associated energies. Two other materials commonly found in kitchens, glass and china or earthenware, are also included below.

Iron and Steel

Iron is one of the most common elements found on earth, and is thought to be necessary to life in trace amounts for most living organisms. Cast iron, one of the most common forms of iron found in the kitchen, is made of iron, carbon, silicon, and trace amounts of manganese. Steel is another common form of iron, alloyed with carbon to strengthen and harden it, along with other trace elements such as tungsten. Magically, iron is believed to deflect magic and psychic energy and increase physical strength, making it a common choice for making protective charms and talismans, or including iron filings in amulet bags and gris-gris pouches. People of various cultures have carried nails, keys, and other iron-made items with them as protective and defensive talismans. Iron nails used to be hammered above doors and windows to prevent entry by evil spirits.

If you are looking for a way to incorporate iron into your magical or spiritual work and don't wish to use cookware or utensils, using a piece of hematite is an excellent way to do so. Hematite is a pewter-colored metal used in magical work for grounding and protection. Lodestones, pieces of stone with iron in them that possess a magnetic charge, are also used in magical work, to either draw certain energy toward them and the bearer, or to deflect certain energies away. Either of these on your altar or shrine will lend their energies to your spiritual hearth. Alternatively, you can eat foods high in iron such as dried fruit, dark green vegetables, nuts, whole grains, and red meat, among others.

In myth and story, blacksmiths and ironworkers often possess a certain level of magical power or defense against evil magics. The defensive and luck-bringing properties of the horseshoe are derived from its iron, as well as its creation by a blacksmith.

Iron and steel are used magically for defense, protection, grounding, strength, energy, willpower, and courage.

Copper

Copper is an excellent conductor, and cooking pots and pans are often entirely or partially made of this metal. Traditionally, copper is associated with Venus, the Roman goddess of love and beauty. It revitalizes, refreshes, is associated with healing, balances outgoing and incoming energies, and is also associated with attracting money. Just as copper is an electrical conductor, it also conducts magical energy. It makes an excellent metal to have around the hearth and home, as it enhances energies such as harmony, abundance, and attraction of positive energy.

Magically copper can be used for work regarding kindness, fertility, peace, harmony, arts-related undertakings, and friendship.

Aluminum

One of the most abundant metals on earth, aluminum is naturally found in several stones such as garnets and staurolite. Aluminum is usually anodized for use as pots and pans. It is a very dense metal, despite its lightness.

As one of the more recent metals, it does not have as many magical associations with it as classical metals such as copper or iron do. Modern associations are travel, communication, and other subjects associated with mental activity. As aluminum is very resistant to corrosion, it may also be used to enhance staying power or permanency and to resist nonbeneficial change.

Tin and Pewter

Tin is most often found in the form of pewter. Modern pewter is tin alloyed with antimony, but older pewter alloyed the tin with lead and copper. Used for making cups and plates and other housewares, pewter is also commonly used for small figurines and jewelry. (Interestingly, Mexican pewter is in fact made of aluminum alloyed with other metals, not tin.)

Magical associations for tin and pewter include business success, legal issues, wisdom, growth, success, healing, and abundance.

Porcelain, China, and Earthenware

These ceramic-based materials are all made from clay and kaolin clay bases with various other materials added to them to create certain effects. They are usually glazed to make them watertight. Clay is an earth-based material, and so these items carry the basic associations of abundance, stability, and fertility.

Glass

Glass is basically melted and fused silicon dioxide, with various minerals added to provide stability. Pyrex contains boron; lead glass or crystal contains lead to increase light's refraction to cause a sparkling effect. Silicon dioxide is found naturally as sand or quartz, both also associated with the element of earth and therefore with the energies of stability and abundance. The quartz category covers many of the stones commonly used in New Age practice such as agate, jasper, and onyx, as well as the translucent stones commonly referred to as quartz. In general, quartz stones are associated with energy, healing, and protection, among others for particular stones.

Ethics, Intent, and Magic in the Kitchen

Cooking in itself is a creative activity. It's also one of the most common activities in the modern kitchen, and therefore one of the most natural methods through which we can express our spirituality, and practice our hearthcraft for the good of our families and homes.

This brings us to the issue of ethics. The subject of ethics was raised in Chapter 2 with the discussion about values and how they can help you define your home-based spirituality. Here we'll address the ethically sticky and confusing issue of cooking for others with spiritual and/or magical intent.

In modern religions such as Wicca, it is generally accepted that attempting to affect someone else through magical or other means without their knowledge or consent is an infringement upon their privacy and expression of free will, and that spells or rituals designed to change someone's status or outlook without their okay is a bad thing. There are other magic-based paths that do not operate under this particular moral restriction. Hearthcraft, however, is not specifically magic-based, nor a religion. Nor does it seek to deliberately alter an individual's position or status for the gain or benefit of the practitioner, or even for the individual being affected. What hearthcraft does do, however, is take full advantage of the open-ended opportunity to generally pass along wishes for peace, health, and happiness.

How does this differ from attempting to manipulate someone with magic? Well, first of all, infusing your kitchen activity with positive energy through channeling Divine love via your spiritual hearth or inviting positive energy into your home isn't manipulating those who live in your home or who visit it as guests. If you prepare food with nonspecific love, then those who consume the food and that love benefit from it in their own way. The key thing to remember is that by serving food made with love, those who eat it have the *opportunity* to absorb the energy that is enhancing it along with the energy provided by the physical component of the meal. They do not automatically do so. Their personal energy has the *choice* to accept the loving energy in your food and home or not.

> *If you bake a cake for someone you like with the intent of creating a love-spell to make them fall in love with you, that classifies as manipulation and interference. If you make a cake for someone you like with the intent of baking the best cake you possibly can, with the hopes that the display of your culinary skill impresses them and perchance may contribute to their overall feelings of admiration for you, that qualifies as noninterference.*

Perhaps this feels like splitting hairs. What it comes down to, however, is that you are not seeking to manipulate anyone by making food with love.

So how do you use spiritual or magical intent in the kitchen? Well, for a start, you can use rituals (and here the word "ritual" is used in the sense of short mental and spiritual preparations before you begin) to help improve your own ability to cook. You can attract as much successful and encouraging energy from your hearth as possible, and direct it into the food you prepare. You can use mindfulness (see Chapter 6) and invocations to improve your ability to plan, prepare, cook, and serve meals (see Chapter 10). And above all, you can cook mindfully, keeping the goal of caring for those who will consume your meal clearly in your mind. Chapter 9 looks at the relationship between food and spirituality in greater depth.

Kitchen Folklore

This is one of the fun things about doing research into home-based customs: discovering the traditions and folklore associated with domestic activity. Here's a series of domestic customs you can use to help enhance your awareness of the spiritual nature of your activity.

- ✦ Stir the contents of pots and bowls clockwise to attract positive energy, or stir counterclockwise to banish things. Use one or the other according to the needs of your home or family at the time.
- ✦ Pass items at the table in a clockwise direction to maintain harmonious energy there.
- ✦ If you wish to clear the house of negative energy, clean it beginning at the back door and travel through it room by room in a counter-clockwise direction until you reach the

back door again, then sweep or mop out the door and off the doorstep.

✦ To attract positive energy, clean items with a clockwise motion. This includes dusting, mopping, and scrubbing as well as wiping counters and washing dishes.

✦ Draw a spiritual symbol that has meaning to you (either cultural, religious, or designed by you) with salt water on the windows of your house, and on the front and back doors. Paint these symbols with clear nail polish if you want something a little more permanent.

✦ If you wish to further connect your cooking to your spiritual hearth, draw a spiritual symbol on the inside of the pot or bowl before you use it. A stylized flame is a good basic image to use.

✦ Empower your laundry detergent for purification of any negative energy clinging to clothes. Water has a natural purification effect, but empowering the cleaning substances you use boosts that natural effect. Do the same for your household cleaners.

✦ Running out of salt is said to be bad luck for the posterity of the home. Keep a small packet of salt somewhere to ensure there will always be salt in the house. (This may be one of the origins of the custom of bringing a bottle of wine, a loaf of bread, and a box of salt to a housewarming.)

✦ Hanging braids or wreaths of garlic, onions, or hot peppers will keep your kitchen free of negative energy. Compost them every fall and hang new ones. Never eat them!

- Hanging bunches of dried Indian corn attracts prosperity and abundance.
- Leave an onion or clove of garlic outside below the kitchen window to absorb any negative energy trying to enter the home. You may leave them around the doors to the house as well. Place a new one there every month, or more frequently if the old ones decay faster.

Regular Purification of the Kitchen

Even with the best of intentions and the attempt to live a spiritually fulfilling life free of stress, unhelpful energy collects, and in general the positive atmosphere you strive to maintain can get a bit ragged. As the kitchen is so frequently used, it may require purification more often than other rooms in the house. A string of clumsiness in the kitchen or bad luck in cooking may mean a purification is in order. Remember, your hearth is sacred to begin with, and the need for purification does not mean it has become tainted in any way; it just means a bit of spiritual housecleaning is in order. Refer back to the purification information in Chapter 7 for ideas on how to purify the kitchen and your home in general.

Traditional Tools

What a household used as tools a century ago are no longer the only tools at a hearth-based hedge witch's disposal! There are dozens of tools available to us in the kitchen now. This section briefly touches on traditional tools and proposes contemporary equivalents.

Apart from the cauldron, which has been thoroughly examined and explored previously, there are a handful of other traditional tools that are or have been used in magical and spiritual work.

The *knife* is a symbol of air or fire, depending on what Western occult tradition you subscribe to, and in some paths is commonly used in a symbolic fashion. The partner to this tool is the *bolline*, a knife used for actual physical cutting and slicing in a ritual context for things such as herbs, carving wood, and so forth. The bolline sometimes has a white handle or a curved blade, while the knife is generally dark-handled and has a straight blade with two edges. Sometimes it is sharpened, sometimes it is left dull to demonstrate that it is a metaphysical tool. Of course, the last thing you need is a knife in the kitchen that you can't use. As hearthcraft is practical, it makes more sense to recognize the spiritual associations of the knives you do use. Knives are generally associated with action, decisiveness, resolve, and confidence.

Another traditional tool is the *wand*. The wand is either a symbol of fire or air (depending on what your belief concerning the knife is, the wand is assigned to the other). Fairy tales feature fairies and sorceresses with magical wands that transform and enchant; tales of wizards and druids feature staves. Both the wand and the staff are symbolic of the same thing. Staves tend to be associated with solidity and grounding as well, reflecting the world tree and the *axis mundi* found in shamanic societies. The obvious modern tool that parallels the wand is the wooden spoon, a tool of transformation and blending.

Another ubiquitous magical symbol is that of the *broom*. Like the staff, it symbolizes grounding, but it also symbolizes the spiritual flights taken seeking knowledge from other spirits and worlds. The broom is said to be a union of the female and male symbols of brush and staff, and as such was used in fertility ceremonies, festivals, and rituals, especially to encourage crops to grow. In more modern magical use, it is used to sweep the energy of a place clean of negativity. In this capacity it is sometimes termed a *besom*, and often kept apart from the everyday broom used to sweep up crumbs and dirt of the floor. In hearthcraft, as every act is a spiritual act, using the everyday broom is a magical act in and of itself. The floor and the energy get swept clean together.

Modern Convenience: Using Appliances for Magic and Spiritual Work

One of the most memorable workshops I've ever attended was given by author Dorothy Morrison. She was talking about making use of the tools you have at hand, and pulled out a food processor to make incense before our eyes. She joked about explaining to Customs why she traveled with the appliance and the audience laughed, but it was something that I found intriguing. Why didn't more magical practitioners use modern equipment in their work? What was it that held them back?

Not long afterwards I bought myself a coffee grinder specifically for making incense. It does a wonderful job grinding resins in particular, which can be finicky to grind by hand in a mortar and pestle, getting sticky with the heat generated by the friction of the grinding or popping out of the mortar when the grains crack. The coffee grinder did the trick. The practicality and efficiency demonstrated by Dorothy was an eye-opener.

I am not necessarily advocating the use of appliances in magical or spiritual practice. I am simply listing them and their alternate uses or energies, as they currently exist in many kitchens. If you do not have some of them, you're not missing out on anything. I'm not a big appliance-fan myself; I like doing things simply. That said, there are a lot of things in our kitchens that we take for granted like the coffeepot, the kettle, and the microwave, and while they may not be traditional tools, you may not have considered them as possibilities for contemporary magical tools either. However, as hearthcraft is about practicality, there's no reason to avoid things you could be using in your daily practice. Why should only certain kitchen activities or tools be spiritual or creative? Why can't we employ electric fryers and stand mixers?

The main argument against using modern kitchen appliances for magic is that the use of electricity somehow disrupts or alters the magic. To each his or her own, but I have rarely found that the electricity running through the wires of my home affects the rituals or spiritual work I do in the rooms made by those walls. The second argument that is sometimes given is that the individual who objects to them feels that he is somehow cheating if an appliance is used. Allow me to stress again that hearthcraft is about practicality. There is no point to making more work for yourself by doing it "the old-fashioned way."

In a different light, however, if you wish to celebrate something by offering up the time and energy it requires to do something without the aid of modern technology in the kitchen, more power to you. It can be a wonderful, meditative experience.

At the very least, recognizing your appliances and kitchen tools as partners in your daily life provides you with yet another opportunity to take advantage of the energies of your environment. Being aware of what is around you and how you use the tools at your disposal allows you to remain more in control of your environment. Becoming familiar with their specific energies further provides you with the opportunity to use them with awareness and precision, thereby enhancing your spiritual experience and broadening or deepening the complex web of energies that make up your hearth and home.

There is one caveat to be applied to using your everyday appliances for magical and spiritual purposes: you can't always use them again for cooking if you've used them to grind or blend something nonconsumable. Take a small food processor or coffee grinder used to make incense, for example. No matter how you scrub, essential oils and resin powder might not come out. If you intend to use small appliances such as these for magical and spiritual-related work, invest in a secondhand machine to devote to that purpose only for the sake of health and safety.

Understanding that every tool you use possesses its own energy is the first step toward gaining a better understanding of how the energy of your kitchen is produced and affected.

How to begin? Well, a good way to do it is to start off by blessing each major appliance in your kitchen. This isn't quite as insane as it sounds. As human beings, we tend to project personalities onto machines because we relate better to things that we perceive as having identities. By recognizing the appliances as participants in your activities at hearth and in home, you formally acknowledge their energies. If you wish to go so far as giving them names, do so. Anything that gives the appliance more of a recognized presence in your kitchen will help.

Your appliances and how they work impact your life in ways you often don't recognize until you lose the use of them through a power failure or system failure of the individual machine. When this happens our reaction is usually a negative one, born of frustration, which is understandable. That negative reaction impacts the energy of your home, however, and it is regrettable if the only conscious response you demonstrate toward appliances and their uses is a negative one.

Take a look around your kitchen and make note of the appliances you use every day. The refrigerator is always on; the stove is at your disposal; the toaster, coffee-maker, and microwave are almost omnipresent in today's kitchens. What if, when you used them, you consciously applied their energy in a positive fashion to the overall energy of your kitchen, your home, and your life?

By taking a moment to formally recognize an appliance, you are signaling to both your own mind and spirit that it is a valued element of your everyday life, and to the energy of the appliance as well. This isn't the place to go into a long discourse about the validity of energy produced by machinery and technological devices as compared to the energy produced by organic and natural-sourced objects; suffice it to say that everything has an energy signature to it, and that energy affects the environment in which the object finds itself. The mechanical-based energy of a toaster oven may be a bit more difficult to grasp and incorporate into your conscious everyday use than the energy of herbs or other symbols, but it is a perfectly legitimate energy. Again, it seems somewhat self-defeating to ignore the modern tools at our disposal when we are seeking to create a spiritually, emotionally, and physically nourishing hearth-centered spiritual practice.

A good place to start is by formally recognizing the major players in your kitchen, the ones that sit on your counters and are used daily or several times each week. One way of doing this is by blessing them (see p. 166). (see p. 166) Think of blessing the appliance as a way of initializing their energy in a positive manner, and weaving it into the overall atmosphere of your hearth.

As an example, let's look at the bread machine. I'm focusing on this instead of the oven because it's a very specific small appliance, whereas the stove and oven tend to be more central in the kitchen. Apart from using a bit more electricity, the bread machine isn't much different from mixing and leaving bread to rise the traditional way. However, it can also be argued that with less input from you, less hands-on activity, you're divorcing yourself further from the potential to imbue your resulting bread product with more magic and or energy. When making bread for specific magical or spiritual purposes, yes, I make it entirely by hand. But for everyday bread, I use the machine, and by blessing the appliance itself and the ingredients as I place them in the pan I'm maximizing the potential for hearth magic on a daily basis. As a result of a physical condition I am slowly losing strength in my hands and therefore I can see that in the near future I will need to use the machine for mixing and kneading even bread for ritual use, and when that happens I'll be fine with it because I recognize that it's the intent and the recognition of the machine itself as a participating element within my hearth and home practice that is key.

Another essential kitchen aid that you probably overlook when you think of tools is your cookbook or recipe file. This does not mean a published cookbook, but rather the binder or folder of recipes you've collected over the years, with the notes scribbled to yourself in the margins or the back of the papers, photocopies and hastily handwritten scraps of paper, pages torn from magazines, recipes printed from websites, tattered recipe cards stained with vanilla extract and coffee and tomato paste. If you stuff these recipes inside the front cover of your main published cookbook or have them loose somewhere, treat yourself to a scrapbook or a sturdy three-ring binder and a set of transparent sheet protectors. The latter is ideal, because the sheet protectors can not only be wiped off when you stir the soup a bit too enthusiastically, but you can slip notes inside them as well.

Your cookbook is paralleled by the book of shadows or grimoire in exclusively spiritual practices. A book of shadows is a place where you can note down things you've tried, changes to spells, records of rituals, recipes and so forth. Your cookbook is another form of this. Arrange it in a way that makes sense to you. Generally recipe collections are arranged by type of dish—appetizer, main dish, one-pot meals, beverages, desserts, and so forth—but if you have another method of organizing your recipes by all means use it.

Keep a kitchen journal as well, one in which you can note down prayers, invocations, information, or nonfood recipes related to your spiritual practice.

Blessing Your Appliances

This is a simple and straightforward act that can be done on a regular basis to help maintain the positive charge to the appliance's energy, tie it into the harmonious energy of the kitchen, and keep it happy. No supplies are needed for this, although if you feel it necessary or preferable you can use a small bowl or cup of plain water, or water with a pinch of salt added to it.

Note that this isn't a cleansing or a purification, simply a blessing. If you sense that it is required, do a purification before the blessing. You may feel the need to do a purification the first time you do this blessing, and not again.

The following instructions use the refrigerator as an example. To perform the blessing on another appliance, simply replace the name and the purpose/use.

1. Stand before the appliance. Touch it with your hands and allow yourself to sense its energy by opening yourself to whatever feelings or sensations the appliance may raise in you. The appliance may "feel" hot, cold, active, passive, slow, fast, eager, aloof, or anything else.

2. When you feel that you have a sense of the appliance's energy and/or personality, say:

Refrigerator,
Thank you for keeping our food fresh and cool.
Thank you for being part of our lives.
I bless you.

3. If you wish, you can draw a symbol on it in plain water, water with a pinch of salt in it, or with a dry finger. The symbol can be anything you feel is appropriate. A good default symbol is a circle, representing harmony. Or perhaps you may wish to use something like a stylized flame, to represent the energy of the hearth of the home.

If you have difficulty sensing the energy of the appliance, consider what each one does in the kitchen and consciously associate it with a similar energy. For example, sugar is sweet, and thus may be associated with friendship, harmony, love. Why not try it with a KitchenAid standalone mixer? It combines separate ingredients into one harmonious entity of dough, so perhaps you may associate it with community, harmony, and active work. Cake tins may symbolize pleasure, celebration, and so forth. Your teapot may represent health, love, support, comfort, and peace.

If you wish, you can do the same for the areas of your kitchen: breakfast nook, pantry, cupboard, and so forth. Don't overlook the contents of your kitchen cupboards. Cleaning supplies, china, dinnerware, and silverware are all easily blessed and/or empowered for harmony and other positive things such as health. Bless the entries into the kitchen too, the doorways and arches or passages into the rest of the house.

On the Magical Nature of Everyday Items

As you have learned in this book, hearthcraft is a practical practice. Here is a small selection of modern kitchen appliances and utensils and comments upon their use in the modern kitchen, and their impact on spiritual practice. Look at your major appliances, small countertop appliances, and other kitchen tools and utensils. What kind of energy do they carry? What sort of things do they symbolize for you? Here are some suggested associations to help you out if you can't pin down a definable energy.

- **Knife sharpener:** focus
- **Can opener:** removing barriers, moving past obstacles
- **Bread machine:** comfort, foundation, abundance
- **Coffee grinder:** focus, heightened awareness, energy
- **Handheld mixer, standalone mixer:** gentle but firm blending of disparate thoughts or energies
- **Espresso machine:** intensity
- **Milk frother:** play, thought, light-heartedness
- **Mandoline:** evenness, precision
- **Crockpot:** slow and steady union

Explore your kitchen cupboards and drawers, and see what you can assign to the utensils and small appliances you find. Patricia Telesco's delightful *Magick Made Easy* can help you think up associations for household items and objects.

Kitchen Activity

Remember that any activity taking place in the kitchen contributes to the energy of the hearth. Likewise, any activity in the kitchen also benefits from the energy of the spiritual hearth. Doing crafts, homework, and other activities in the kitchen helps tie them into the energy that surrounds the home, and can have a beneficial effect upon the results.

Chapter Nine

The Spiritual Aspect of Food

This chapter is divided into two parts. The first part looks at the relationship between food and spirituality. The second half focuses on simple hearth-based or hearth-associated dishes and recipes.

People who practice home-based spirituality generally believe that everyday actions reinforce their spirituality, and that their spirituality is reflected in their everyday actions. They often engage in recycling, reusing, composting, and caring for the environment. Despite this, food is often overlooked as one of the key elements in that spiritual practice.

Food and food-related activities play a significant role in our lives, and yet other than foods associated with holidays, we rarely think of it as having a spiritual connection. Food is a very physical thing, and as such we often forget that it has a place within our spiritual lives as well. Recognizing the spiritual aspect of food offers us something informal that we can do to touch our spirituality on a daily basis.

Here's an exercise that can reveal some interesting facts about your eating habits: For one week, keep a journal of what food you prepare and what you consume. Note down the following:

+ The ingredients
+ Total time spent assembling and cooking
+ Time spent eating
+ Where you ate it
+ How much was eaten, and how much was left over
+ If the leftovers were eaten the next day or in days following
+ What spiritual practices you engaged in while you did any/all of the above (what prayers did you say, did you specifically add an ingredient or herb with a magical intent, did you leave an offering to a god or spirit, and if you did so, when?)

This collection of information can teach you a great deal about how much weight you give to various steps of the food preparation and consumption process.

The Energy of Food

When you handle something, part of your personal energy is transferred to it. Your base energy is affected by your emotional state, which acts as a lens or a filter through which your personal energy passes and is thereby affected by it.

This is important to remember all the time (it's one of the reasons why you're not supposed to handle sacred objects without being properly prepared) but it's particularly important to remember when you handle food.

The common saying is that *you are what you eat*, but it is also true to say that you *eat what you are*, or more precisely, who you were when you prepared your meal. And if you're eating a meal prepared by someone else, you're consuming some of their energy, too. (This may make you look at eating out in a different way, especially if you do it a lot because you think you can't cook, or it seems inconvenient, or you don't enjoy your kitchen.)

The spiritual dimension of food and food-related activity nourishes the soul through the exchange of energy. Preparing and consuming food spiritually is an act of appreciation for the here and now. Consuming food spiritually can involve thinking about the food's sources, its connections, its associations to the season, its place in your life, and the impact its energy has on yours, among other things. The spiritual appreciation of food is subtle, but it nourishes and strengthens your connection to the spiritual aspect of the world around you.

Everyone eats. It's one of the basic physical needs mentioned in Chapter 1. A personal spiritual connection to your food gives it another dimension beyond the basic physical relationship of fuel to consumer, however. The very least food can do is deliver the basic calorie package with its vitamins and nutrients to the consumer. It only makes sense to enhance it by handling it with awareness at every step of the process in order to maximize its spiritual potential. Why would you not want to provide the maximum amount of good the food could do for those to whom you serve it? Why would you not use food as a spiritual expression and mode of communication? Because your energy affects food at every stage of the process of preparation and consumption, it's important to be aware of your energy while you do it.

As touched on in Chapter 8, there are ethical issues that surround using food as an undeclared vehicle of change for people other than yourself; it may be interpreted as magical manipulation and a trespass upon someone's free will, without the subject's consent. This is a good rule of thumb to keep in mind. However, I'm not talking about baking a batch of cookies to stealthily coerce your boss into giving you a raise; I'm talking about the simple fact that how you prepare and consume food has a spiritual impact upon you and those you feed.

Food does possess its own energy, and generally this will be the predominant energy it carries. The energy of every person who has handled it will add to it, however, modifying and shaping the innate energy to various extents. An offering of food to deity is an offering of the food's energy, but also a sacrifice of the physical benefit you might obtain from it. (Theoretically the spiritual reward for the offering outweighs the sacrificed physical benefit!)

Gather, Prepare, and Eat with Awareness.

What is *awareness*? It means being in the moment and acting mindfully. (To refresh your memory, you may want to look back at Chapter 6.) By clearing the mind and focusing on each movement and action one makes during the process, you can gain a better understanding of the spiritual nourishment provided by interacting with food. On a practical level, it also relaxes the mind and body which in turn facilitates the consumption and digestion of the food, as well as deepening our appreciation for the taste and texture.

Eating simply to keep us alive denies the spiritual aspect of the act. By eating with awareness, we create the opportunity for that spiritual connection to re-emerge in our lives.

Food is such a presence in our everyday lives that it's easy to forget that it's a spiritual thing as well. To add dimension to the spiritual aspect of your relationship with food and eating, try the following:

+ When you plan a meal, think about the various sources and origins of the different foods that you intend to involve.
+ Consider how seasonally available food reflects the energy of the turning year, and how internalizing that energy by eating the food in turn affects you.
+ Take the opportunity to prepare and eat seasonally available foods, and note down how your relationship with the season's energy is affected.
+ Take the time to prepare your food in a relaxed, aware, and focused manner.
+ Do not multitask while eating; take the time to consume that food in a relaxed manner, savoring each bite and appreciating the energy.

Like other work in the kitchen, if your mind wanders when you set out to prepare food in a spiritual frame of mind or if you have difficulty focusing on the spiritual aspect, *don't stress about it.* Try touching or standing at your altar or shrine for a moment before preparing food to serve as a visual reminder that it is a spiritual act. Lighting candles on the table or saying grace or a blessing can remind everyone of the spiritual aspect of eating, too. At the very least, being in a neutral or positive frame of mind is key to creating and consuming food that is spiritually nourishing as well as physically nourishing.

How you approach food reflects and reinforces your spirituality, so you may as well engage with it consciously instead of just eating because you have to. There's a lot of extra benefit to be obtained from looking at food in a spiritual light. Nutritionist and spiritual counselor Deborah Kesten suggests that eating disorders and unhealthy relationships with food reflect a spiritual disconnection between a person's soul and food. Her thoughts on the spiritual aspect of food and eating are thought-provoking, and if the topic interests you, you might enjoy reading her book Feeding the Body, Nourishing the Soul.

+ Do not cook if you are angry, resentful, or afraid. The energy transfers to the food; the energy creates a less than supportive environment.
+ Always sit down to eat. Honor the food and the people eating it by taking the time to sit and consume it.
+ Before you begin to prepare food, take a moment to take a deep breath and exhale with awareness to bring yourself into the moment.

✦ To help you focus, bless the kitchen by lighting a candle as a representative of the sacred fire, itself a representation of the Goddess. Another alternative is to flick drops of water around the kitchen with your fingers, if that works for you. You can put a pinch of salt in the water if you like.

Food and the Seasonal Cycle

In our global village society, we can eat strawberries in January and cherries in November. We've forgotten that once upon a time people had to seize the opportunity to enjoy seasonal food within a limited time frame. As different fruits and vegetables became available, the changing of the seasons was reinforced in the mind of the community. The energies felt during the different seasons can also affect the energy of your spiritual heart and in your home, so paying attention to them is a good way to further nourish your spiritual hearth and keep your home a place of comfort and renewal.

You can explore the seasonal and spiritual aspect of food today by shopping regularly at a farmer's market. Week by week, the produce available will vary in supply and quality. By familiarizing yourself with what is available at different times of the year in your region you can gain a better understanding of those energies and how they impact the energy of the food you prepare. Bring a selection of that seasonal produce home regularly and prepare those items, sensing their energies as you touch them and taste them.

The second half of this chapter will include a focus on bread-making. Here's a concrete example of how making bread can be perceived as a spiritual activity. I often use fresh herbs from my garden to flavor bread, but even more than the inclusion of seasonal produce, the act of mixing and baking it makes it a spiritual act for me. After mixing, it must be left to rise, which reminds me that patience is required to see labor rewarded, a theme closely associated with harvest festivals. The kneading reminds me that effort is necessary for a positive result. Finally, the baking exemplifies the alchemy of transformation, the long-term goal of spiritual development. The eating of the bread reminds me to appreciate the simpler things in life, and also allows me to feel pride in my skill.

Honor the spiritual energy of the food you eat by acknowledging its presence and participation in your own spiritual practice. Look upon the food you prepare and consume as a way to interact with the natural flow of energy, and respect your time spent eating food as an essential element within your ongoing dialogue with your spirituality. Like other natural objects, food has a great deal to teach us about ourselves and our relationship with the world around us. Eating and preparing food offers us the chance to touch nature and celebrate our spirituality on a daily basis, without taking extra formal action. By simply listening to what the energy of food has to say to us while you consume it with awareness, you can appreciate the flow of energy and the affirmation of life, and further expand your home-based spiritual practice.

Recipes

The recipes in the second half of this chapter focus mainly on very traditional hearth-associated dishes. This is not meant to indicate that only traditional foods can function as spiritual meals or in ritual environments. Rather, traditional dishes tend to focus on very fundamental issues such as comfort and basic needs. These recipes aren't going to cover a very wide range of dishes, either. Instead, we'll focus on two very basic foods that are and were easily made at the hearth: bread, and stews and casseroles. These two kinds of dishes represent some of the very best things associated with the hearth: harmony; slow blending of flavor and disparate elements; warmth; nourishment; and ease of preparation.

If you are interested at all in cooking on an open hearth, be it in a fireplace or outdoors, an excellent source to refer to is William Rubel's *The Magic of Fire: Hearth Cooking—One Hundred Recipes for the Fireplace or Campfire.*

Bread

Bread is one of the essential basic foods of the Western world and has been one for centuries. I freely admit that I now use a bread machine. I only acquired one after two decades of making bread by hand because I wanted to start making all our family bread at home, and while kneading is something meditative and therapeutic it does take time, and that's not something I have a lot of. I also don't have a surface in my kitchen that is low enough for me to do it comfortably, and my hands are losing the strength with which to knead properly.

That having been said, there are times when I still make bread by hand, especially for ritual or spiritual use (the recipe for herb bread in *The Way of the Green Witch* is an example). And while I sometimes do use the baking step of the machine, I now tend to take the dough out after the first rise, punch it down, and shape it in loaf pans for a second rise and bake them in the oven. I prefer the texture I get that way.

BASIC TRADITIONAL BREAD RECIPE

This recipe comes from my friend Janice, and she has given me permission to share it with you. It's a very straightforward and easy technique. Most bread is easy; it just seems overwhelming for beginners. If you have a bread machine, this is not the recipe for you. It's worth trying by hand to have the experience. This recipe makes 1 large or 2 small loaves.

You will need:

+ 2 cups (1 pint) warm water
+ 2 tablespoons sugar (or honey)
+ 1 tablespoon traditional yeast (NOT fast-rise or bread machine yeast)
+ Whole wheat flour
+ White flour
+ ½ teaspoon salt
+ Olive or other cooking oil

1. Put 2 cups of warm water in a large bowl (preferably glass or ceramic) and stir in the sugar or honey until dissolved.
2. Sprinkle the yeast into the water. If using traditional yeast, wait 5 to 10 minutes for the yeast to "prove."

3. Mix in about 2 cups of whole wheat flour. Stir until there are no big lumps. Now add more whole wheat flour little by little, mixing in well, until your mixing spoon (preferably wood) will stand up on its own in the middle of the bowl for a couple of seconds before falling over. It should have a consistency sort of like cake batter.

4. Set in a warm (25–30°C/around 80°F is ideal) place to rise for at least 2 hours. You may cover it with a damp, smooth cloth or not, as you prefer. (Jan says she got tired of washing cloths embedded with sticky dough, and has no problem with the sponge rising uncovered.)

5. Add salt. Mix in as much white flour as the dough will take, until it forms a ball, and stops sticking to your hands.

6. Sprinkle table or countertop with flour. Knead for at least 5 full minutes, adding flour as necessary to keep the dough "dry" and not sticky.

7. Thoroughly oil a loaf pan.

8. Form the dough into a loaf shape. Put it in the loaf pan bottom side up, then turn it over (this is a quick way to get most of the top of the loaf oiled.) Brush any parts that are still dry with a little more oil. (If making two small loaves, separate into two equal lumps, form into loaves, place in oiled pans.)

9. Set back in a warm place and allow to rise again. Within 45 minutes to 1 hour, you should have a full-sized loaf in the pan.

10. Bake for 30 to 35 minutes at 375°F.

11. Take the baked loaf out of the pan as soon as you can safely handle it, and cool on a wire rack for at least 30 minutes. (Otherwise the bottom of the loaf goes all mushy.)

BASIC LOAF RECIPE FOR BREAD MACHINES

Here's a basic bread recipe for the machine. I use all whole wheat flour, but it works well with white all-purpose flour or a blend of the two in any proportion as well. I add the egg because I find it gives the bread a bit more stability, but it works just as well without it. If you don't use the egg, you may end up using a bit less flour.

This recipe makes about a 2½ pound loaf. My machine makes a maximum loaf size of 2 pounds, so I cut off a third of the dough after the first rise and allow it to rise separately, and then bake it as a small round cottage loaf on a baking sheet. Alternatively, if your machine has a smaller capacity cut down on the yeast by a teaspoon, and the flour by about a half to a full cup (start off with three cups of flour and add more as the dough mixes to make a nice smooth ball, then make a note of how much flour you used in total).

You will need:

+ ¾ cup of milk
+ ¾ cup warm water
+ 1 egg (optional)
+ 1½ tablespoons of honey
+ 1½ teaspoons of salt
+ 4 cups whole wheat flour
+ 1 tablespoon of yeast

1. Put the ingredients into the pan in this order (or in the order directed by your machine manufacturer if it doesn't follow the basic liquids first/flour/yeast order).
2. Select the basic sandwich loaf setting and press start.

BASIC SCONES

Scones are like a cup of tea: they're easy to make, are comforting to eat, and they're quick and easy to serve to unexpected guests or just to make for yourself on a morning when you need a touch of comfort. They make excellent morning snacks or afternoon break treats.

I prefer my scones without anything extra in them, but this recipe adapts well to the inclusion of raisins, currants, nuts with a pinch of cinnamon, or chopped dried fruit. Use about a half cup of whatever you're adding.

I recommend using whole milk, but if you have a full or partly skimmed on hand use that. If you use a lower-fat milk add a bit of cream or a dollop of yogurt for richness. If you want a sweeter scone, use more honey to taste.

You will need:

+ 2 cups whole wheat flour, plus extra for hands and baking sheet
+ 3 teaspoons baking powder
+ ½ teaspoon salt
+ ¼ cup margarine or unsalted butter (at room temperature)
+ ¾ cup milk (whole, preferably)
+ 1–2 tablespoons honey
+ 1 egg

1. Preheat oven to 400°F.
2. In a large bowl, whisk together the flour, baking powder, and salt.
3. With a pastry cutter or two forks, cut in the margarine or butter.
4. Mix the honey into the milk, and add it to the flour and butter mixture.
5. Beat the egg lightly with a fork (I do it in the measuring cup that held the milk and honey, so as to blend in the last bit of honey sticking to the bottom) and add to the batter. Stir to combine.
6. Lightly flour the middle of a baking sheet. Scrape the batter onto the sheet. With lightly floured hands shape it into a rough disc shape.
7. Score the disc into eight wedges. Don't separate them, just cut the dough about halfway to three-quarters of the way through.
8. Bake in preheated oven for 20 to 25 minutes. Remove from oven and allow them to cool for 5 minutes on the baking sheet. Cut through the scores to fully separate the wedges. Serve warm with butter, jam, or clotted (Devonshire) cream.

These scones can also be made as individual scones. Instead of turning the dough out onto the baking sheet, flour a counter or pastry board and turn the batter out on to it. With floured hands, pat the dough down to about an inch and a half thick. Cut out individual scones using a round cutter (I like one about two and a half inches across). When you press the cutter into the dough, do not twist it; the scones won't rise as high. Use a flat or offset spatula to lift the scones from the counter onto the baking sheet. Reroll dough lightly and continue cutting scones out until there isn't enough to fill the cutter. Roll the last bit of dough into a ball with your hands and pat it down to approximately the same height as the cut scones, and place it on the sheet. Bake for eighteen to twenty minutes, watching the scones carefully.

FOCACCIA

I had to include this recipe because the word *focaccia* is also derived from the Latin word *focus*, meaning hearth or center of the home. In essence, then, focaccia is a hearth-bread. To the ancient Romans, *panis focacius* was a flat bread baked in the ashes of the hearth. We know it as Italian flatbread, but many cultures have a version of it.

This is the basic version I make. It is extremely flexible and adaptable. If you have a favorite pizza dough recipe you can use that, and indeed I use this as my pizza dough as well. I often split a third of it off to make focaccia and use the other two-thirds as a base for homemade pizza. It is best eaten directly out of the oven; it loses something of its personality if kept and eaten the next day.

I use half all-purpose and half whole wheat flour, but you can use any combination you like. Other toppings you can use include fresh minced onion, garlic, chopped olives, and sundried tomatoes; the only limit is your imagination. If you wish, you can knead the toppings into the dough itself instead; just remember to drizzle the top with the olive oil and sprinkle it with salt.

This recipe makes two focaccias or pizzas of approximately twelve inches in diameter, and is easily halved for a single focaccia.

You will need:

+ ½ cup warm water
+ 1 tablespoon honey
+ 2 teaspoons yeast
+ 1½ teaspoons salt
+ 4½ cups flour
+ 2 tablespoons olive oil
+ Warm water

Toppings:

+ Olive oil
+ ½ cup freshly grated Parmesan cheese
+ Kosher sea salt
+ Oregano
+ Parsley
+ Basil

1. In a small bowl or cup, mix water and honey; sprinkle yeast on top. Allow to sit for 8 to 10 minutes until yeast is foamy.
2. In a large bowl, whisk together 2 cups of the flour and the salt. Add yeast mixture and oil, and mix thoroughly.
3. Add warm water and flour alternately while mixing, a bit at a time, until the dough forms a ball and pulls away from the walls of the bowl.

4. Turn dough out onto a floured surface and knead the rest of the flour in. Knead for about 5 minutes until smooth and elastic.

5. Lightly oil a clean bowl and place the dough in it, turning it to coat it with the oil. Cover it with a damp cloth and leave in a warm place to rise for an hour until double in size.

6. Preheat oven to 425°F. Turn dough out and punch it down. Cut the dough in half, and cover one half while you work with the other. Knead dough briefly, and pat it into a rough circle about three-quarters of an inch thick (or to your preferred thickness).

7. Lightly oil a baking sheet and sprinkle it with cornmeal. Move the dough circle to the sheet. Using your fingers, press indentations into the surface of the dough. Leave it to rise for approximately twenty minutes. If you prefer a flatter bread put it directly in the oven.

8. Brush the surface of the dough with olive oil. Sprinkle it with coarse sea salt. Sprinkle it with ¼ cup of freshly grated Parmesan cheese, and parsley, basil, and oregano to your taste. Repeat with the other focaccia.

9. Bake focaccia at 425°F for twenty minutes, or until golden. Allow to cool until it can be handled, and slice into wedges.

CORN BREAD

Another quick and very easy bread, this is wonderful served with stew or chili. This recipe can be made in a regular 8 by 8-inch square pan or a pie plate, but can also be baked in a skillet or frying pan that is oven safe. Why not try baking it in your cast iron cauldron? Make sure your cauldron is big enough; an 8-inch diameter pot is ideal.

You will need:

+ 2 cups yellow cornmeal (you may substitute up to half the amount of cornmeal with flour)
+ 1 egg (beaten)
+ 1 cup milk
+ ¼ cup oil (vegetable or olive)
+ 1 tablespoon sugar
+ Oil for greasing pan

1. Heat oven to 425°F. Grease the inside of the pan and place it in the oven.
2. In a medium or large bowl, beat the egg and add the milk and oil. Stir in sugar, then cornmeal, just until moistened. The batter should be lumpy—do not overmix.
3. Carefully remove the pan from the oven and pour in the batter. Return the pan to the oven.
4. Bake for 20 to 30 minutes, or until the surface is golden brown and a knife inserted in the center comes out clean. Serve warm.

Stews and Casseroles

These are the ultimate in easily prepared one-dish meals. Hearth-associated foods tend to be easily put together and are often one-dish or -pot affairs.

BEEF STEW

You will notice the absence of potatoes in this recipe. While potatoes are traditionally included in beef stews, my family prefers this served over a bowl of brown rice. If you wish to include potatoes, dice them and add them with the tomato sauce. Serves four.

You will need:

+ Beef stew cubes (approximately 1½ pounds)
+ 1 large onion, chopped
+ 1 clove garlic, finely minced
+ ⅓ cup flour
+ 4 to 5 carrots, scraped and sliced
+ 3 stalks celery, washed and chopped
+ ⅓ cup tomato sauce
+ ½ cup wine (either red or white)
+ 1 cup beef stock
+ Button mushrooms (optional)
+ 2 bay leaves
+ Oregano
+ Basil
+ Salt

- ✦ Pepper
- ✦ Olive oil

1. Toss the beef cubes in a mixing bowl with the flour and salt and pepper.
2. Over medium heat, heat the olive oil in a pot. Add the onion, the carrot, and the celery. Fry until the chopped onion is fragrant and soft. Add the garlic and stir-fry for another minute.
3. Add a bit more olive oil if necessary. Add the floured beef cubes and stir continually, browning the meat.
4. Add the tomato sauce and keep stirring. Pour in the stock and the wine.
5. Add the bay leaves, and the other herbs to taste. Add salt and pepper if necessary.
6. Cover and simmer over minimum heat for at least three hours.

HUNTER'S CHICKEN

Also known as chicken cacciatore, this tomato-chicken stew is best served over egg noodles, although it also tastes wonderful served over brown rice. I prefer to use chicken thighs as they have a richer taste, but chicken breasts may also be used. It serves three to four people.

You will need:

- ✦ Chicken thighs (approximately 2 pounds)
- ✦ Fresh button mushrooms (you may use portobello mushrooms)
- ✦ 1 large onion, chopped

- 1 clove garlic, finely minced
- ⅓ cup flour
- ⅓ cup tomato sauce
- ½ cup wine (either red or white)
- 1 cup chicken stock
- 2 bay leaves
- Oregano
- Basil
- Salt
- Pepper
- Olive oil

1. Chop the chicken into pieces roughly one inch by three inches. Toss in a mixing bowl with the flour and salt and pepper.
2. Over medium heat, heat the olive oil in a pot. Fry the chopped onion till fragrant and soft. Add the garlic.
3. Add a bit more olive oil if necessary. Add the floured chicken and stir continually, browning the meat.
4. Add the tomato sauce and keep stirring. Pour in the stock and the wine.
5. Add the bay leaves, and the other herbs to taste. Add salt and pepper if necessary.
6. Cover and simmer over minimum heat for at least an hour.

PORTOBELLO BEEF CHILI

This is my favorite cold-weather one-pot dish! I suggest serving it with focaccia, but it goes well with any hearty bread, or corn bread.

You will need:

- 2 pounds ground beef
- 4 to 6 large portobello mushrooms
- Red wine (approximately 1 cup, or more to taste)
- 2 onions, sliced
- 2 cans red kidney beans (or two cans mixed beans)
- 2 cans diced tomatoes
- 1 can tomato paste
- Chili powder or dried chilis, to taste
- 2 bay leaves
- Salt
- Pepper
- Olive oil

1. Chop portobello mushrooms into small dice shapes, approximately a half-inch square, and place them in a mixing bowl. Pour the red wine over the mushrooms. Stir occasionally to make sure all the mushrooms have been marinated in the wine. Refrigerate and allow to marinate for at least 2 hours.
2. In a large pot, heat olive oil. Add sliced onions, and fry until fragrant and soft.
3. Add ground beef, and fry until browned. Spoon off any fat.
4. Add tomatoes and tomato paste. Stir.
5. Stir in beans.
6. Stir in mushrooms and red wine. Add bay leaf. Add chilis. Adjust seasoning to taste. Add more red wine if desired.
7. Simmer for at least three hours.

8. Serve with warm focaccia. If desired, grated sharp or extra-old Cheddar may be sprinkled on top of each bowl of chili.

A Final Note on the Relationship Between Food and Spirituality

If you follow a home-based spiritual path, chances are good that you already honor food as more than simply fuel. It is a connection to the natural world, as well as a connection to the network of people who have raised it, harvested it, transported it, packaged it, stocked it, and sold it.

The best course of action is to focus on love. Prepare food with love, serve it with love, and eat it with love. Handle food with love and respect for it, and for your near and dear ones, and it will spiritually nourish and support those who eat it.

Chapter Ten

Crafts, Activities, and Techniques

As the hearth-based hedge witch's path revolves around home and family, a chapter devoted to crafts and techniques through which hearth magic may be shared seems essential! This chapter explores projects you can share with your friends and family, as well as exploring basic techniques found in magical practice that are particularly suited to hearth magic, such as candle magic and herbal magic. These activities and crafts, among many others not included here, are hearth-based in that they have as their goals the enhancement of your home environment, the health and happiness of your home.

Seasonal Collages

This is a great craft that the whole family can engage in. It's particularly good for doing with small children. You can do one per season, or choose holidays throughout the year. When it's finished pin it on the wall or tape it to the fridge.

If you intend to make this an ongoing project, make sure you choose a location that can be more permanent.

This collage can be done any size, but I recommend using the large 22 by 28-inch poster board size to provide plenty of space for images and found objects.

You will need:

+ Poster board (color your choice)
+ Scissors
+ Glue
+ Magazines, flyers, catalogs, old greeting cards, etc.
+ Photographs
+ Found objects related to the season
+ Crayons, markers, colored pencils
+ Blank drawing paper or construction paper

1. From the catalogs, magazines, cards, and flyers cut out images associated with the season (e.g., summer-themed images may include beach balls, ice cream, sandals, sunhats, strawberries, sun, and so forth). Sort through the photographs and choose ones that support the theme of the collage, cutting portions of them out if you wish. Draw pictures or write words on the blank paper and cut them out as well.

2. Begin gluing the images and words on the poster board. You may lay the images out first to find a pattern that pleases you, or you can begin gluing the images wherever you are inspired to glue them and allow the collage to form on its own.

3. Attach found objects (twigs, small stones, grasses, shells, etc.) to the collage. This can be done as an ongoing activity, with found items being added throughout the season as they are discovered.

4. Take the collage down at the next holiday and begin the next collage. The past collages can be dated and kept as a record, although you may wish to store them in garbage bags to protect the found items (if used).

As an alternate approach, you can explore themes or ideas that are meaningful to you through a collaging project like this. It can be inspiring to explore aspects of your spirituality by creating an ancestor collage, or a collage with the theme of harmony or the notion of the sacred flame. If the idea of using a collage to explore your spirituality or inner spirit interests you, you may wish to read Seena B. Frost's book *SoulCollage*.

Homemade Play Dough

This is a nonedible dough that you can play with, or use to make small figures, symbols, and ornaments. If you intend to dry and keep your creations, make sure they're not too thick or large. It's not designed for large-scale projects.

The basic dough is a neutral color, but you can color it by adding drops of food coloring, powdered tempera paint, or a small packet of drink crystals such as Kool-Aid. It keeps well stored in self-sealing sandwich bags in the fridge for anywhere between two and three months.

There are several variations of the recipe for this dough found online and in books of activities for children. Play with the ingredient proportions until you find a variation you like. This variation makes approximately two cups of play dough.

You will need:

+ 2 cups flour
+ ¾ cup salt
+ 2 tablespoons cream of tartar
+ 1 tablespoon oil
+ 2 cups water
+ Food coloring or other coloring agent (optional)

1. In a saucepan over low heat, mix the dry ingredients.
2. In a measuring cup, mix the water and the oil. Add to the dry ingredients over low heat, stirring continually. If you're using a powdered coloring agent, add it now.
3. Stir as the mixture thickens. Remove from heat when the mixture begins to pull away from the sides of the pot and forms a ball.
4. Allow the dough to cool. If you wish to color it with liquid or gel food coloring, separate the dough into as many colors as you intend to make, and add a drop or two of the food coloring to each ball and knead it in.
5. To store the dough, seal it in zip-top plastic bags and press out as much air as possible. Store the bagged dough in the fridge. Allow it to come to room temperature before using it.

6. Your creations can be air dried in a safe place; it will take approximately a week. Set them on a small square of waxed paper and leave them on a windowsill or on top of the fridge, and turn them regularly. If you prefer to dry them in the oven, set them on a foil-lined baking sheet and bake them for at least one hour at approximately 250°F. Thicker objects may dry on the outside and then the interiors may liquefy and run out of a crack; heat them slowly. The resulting hard items will be fragile; handle them carefully.

7. When dry, the objects may be painted and then varnished to help strengthen them.

Herb Magic

When you page through herbal books, magical or otherwise, you will find that most plants are associated with protection and/or love in some way. There is a very simple reason for this: herbs and green things are reflections of the natural world, and these common associations are also two things most desired by humankind, knowingly or unknowingly. Both love and protection are two important themes in hearthcraft. Love doesn't necessarily mean for love spells, or to entice someone else to fall in love with you; this is a very common misconception. As a hearth-based hedge witch, you want your home to be a place filled with love for family and friends. Love of the self is also important, as it signifies acceptance and support of oneself, something that is often rarer than it ought to be.

If working with the energy of herbs interests you, I suggest you take a look at *The Way of the Green Witch* for many ideas incorporating the energies of herbs and other items of the natural world into your spiritual and magical work.

Teas and Brews

Warning!
Make sure you know what you're doing if you plan on making something to drink. Use reliable reference books to identify and prepare herbal medicine or beverages.

The most basic way to make a tea is by steeping fresh or dried plant matter in very hot water, or *infusing* it. The resulting liquid is called an *infusion*. This method is most effective for leaves, flowers, and crushed fruit.

If the plant matter is chunky or dense, as bark, roots, or needles tend to be, then a *decoction* is called for. A decoction is made by actually boiling or heating the plant matter in water for a longer period of time.

For a longer-lasting liquid form, a *tincture* can be made. A tincture is generally also stronger than an infusion. It is made by infusing plant matter in a stable long-lived base such as alcohol or glycerin. Here are some examples of basic infusions and decorations.

+ To make herbal or floral water, place approximately a double handful of your chosen plant matter in a sterilized covered bottle or jar. Pour boiling water over it until it just covers the plant matter. Cover with the lid, shake, and leave to cool and steep. Shake it two or three times weekly. After about ten days strain and store the water in a clean jar or bottle. It will keep in the refrigerator for one to two weeks. If you wish to intensify the scent, steep a new batch of plant matter in the infusion. This can be used as a body splash, or an additive for cleaning water. This also makes a very gentle space purifier when misted around a room.

+ To make herbal vinegar, place a handful of your chosen plant matter in a clean jar with a lid. Pour vinegar over it until it just covers the plant matter. Leave the vinegar to steep in the refrigerator for one to three weeks. Strain the vinegar into a clean bottle and label it with the name and the date. Use herbal vinegar in place of regular vinegar, or as an additive to wash water for floors or windows.

+ To make herbal oils, place a handful of your chosen plant matter in a small saucepan, and pour a cup of light olive or safflower oil over it. Heat the oil and plant matter gently over a low heat for fifteen minutes, then pour oil and plant matter into a clean jar. Cover the jar with a double layer of cheesecloth and fasten with a rubber band. Allow to sit in a sunny spot for ten days to two weeks, then strain oil into a clean bottle, cap, and label with the name and date. Use the oil in cooking (if the plant matter is edible), or to anoint objects, windows, doors, and so forth.

Other ways of using infusions and similar extracts:

+ To make herbal or floral sprays, place a freshly made cooled infusion in a clean spray bottle and mist it into the air. Alternatively, place a few drops of a decoction or tincture into a bottle of clean water and shake to blend. It's not the amount that matters, it's the energy that the drops carry.
+ To make floor washes, add an infusion, drops of decoction or tincture, or drops of essential oil to a bucket of clean water. Mop floor, or dip a clean cloth into the wash water and wipe down walls, doorframes, window ledges, and so forth.
+ For use in baths, add an infusion, decoction, or drops of tincture or oil to your bathwater.

Here are some suggestions for herbal blends that can be used for various applications such as simmering potpourri, sprinkling or sweeping powders, in sealed bottles as talismans, or steeped, strained, and used as anointing potions. If you can't stand the smell of one of these, or know your personal energy doesn't interact well with it, leave it out or find a substitute with a similar energy.

+ **Productive energy:** cinnamon, clove, allspice, ginger
+ **Healing:** vervain, rose, chamomile
+ **Relaxation:** rose, chamomile, lavender

- **Communication:** basil, carnation, lavender
- **Protection:** vervain, rosemary, pinch of salt, clove

Potpourri

There are two kinds of potpourri: dry and wet (or simmering). Dry potpourri is about as simple as you can get: it's a blend of dried herbs, flowers, and spices placed in an open dish to scent the air and allow the energy to gently spread. Simmering potpourri is only marginally more challenging: the potpourri is placed in a pot of water and simmered on the stove. If you've ever mulled wine or apple cider, then you've engaged in a form of simmering potpourri.

BASIC DRY POTPOURRI RECIPE

Don't chop up your plant material; if you begin with it fresh and intend to dry it yourself for your potpourri try to keep the natural oils as unbruised as possible, as these are what give dried flowers and spices their scent. When dry, crumble the plant matter into large bits. The orris root is a fixative, something that will help fix the natural and added essential oils to preserve the scent of the mix longer. As a rule, use two tablespoons of the orris root powder per cup of dry potpourri mix.

You will need:

- Dried herbs
- Dried flowers
- Dried spices

- 6 drops of essential oil per cup of dry mix
- Powdered orris root

1. Place all the dried plant matter (including the powdered orris root) in a bowl and stir with your hands to combine. Sprinkle with the essential oil and stir again.
2. Keep the blend in a closed container for at least two weeks to mellow or ripen; this allows the scents to blend. Open the container and stir it once a day to keep it from going moldy. Even if you think your plant material is perfectly dry, there can sometimes be a drop or two of moisture left in it.
3. When it's ready, put your potpourri in an open container and place it in the area you wish to be affected by the energy.

It's important that you not forget about your dry potpourri once you've set it out. Dust collects in it, and exposure to air and the energy of the room will eventually weaken the energy herbal components. Make a new batch when you feel the energy of the old one has expired. You can bury used potpourri or compost it.

When making a batch of potpourri, it's a nice idea to set a small spoonful of it in a dish on your kitchen or hearth shrine as an offering.

Dry potpourri also makes a good stuffing for herbal pillows, sachets, dolls, and so forth.

POTPOURRI SOAP

One use for dry potpourri is as an additive for soap balls. This makes a gently scented soap that is easy to make, as it uses grated soap bars as a base. Castile soap is olive-oil based and can be found in natural food store or fair-trade shops; if you can't find it use a gentle soap such as Ivory or Dove instead.

You will need:

- ✦ 2 bars of castile soap (or 1 cup of soap flakes)
- ✦ Boiling water (about ⅛ cup)
- ✦ Measuring cup
- ✦ Microwave
- ✦ Rubber gloves
- ✦ Foil-lined tray or baking sheet
- ✦ Chopstick
- ✦ 1 tablespoon of dry potpourri
- ✦ 5 drops of essential oil (optional)

1. If the potpourri has large chunks, crush it into smaller pieces.
2. Grate the bars of soap into a microwave-safe container. Stir one spoonful of boiling water into the soap flakes with the chopstick.
3. Microwave at 80 percent power for ten seconds at a time until the mixture begins to melt and bubble. Remove and stir with the chopstick; if the mixture is too stiff to stick together, add another few drops of boiling water.
4. Add a spoonful of potpourri to the soap mixture and stir. If you wish, add an extra few drops of essential oil to soap and potpourri and stir again.

5. Put on the rubber gloves. Scoop up a small amount of the soap mixture with your fingers and roll or press it into a ball. Place each ball on the foil-lined tray or baking sheet to dry.

SIMMERING POTPOURRI

Simmering potpourri is a more active way of diffusing scent and energy into a space, although it is less permanent. It also adds moisture to the air, making it an excellent winter-time activity. I recommend you keep a small saucepan for potpourri use only, and never use it for food preparation. Essential oils can linger on the finishes of pots and pans.

Dried apple slices and citrus peel make particularly good fixatives for simmering potpourri. Keep the peels from grapefruits or oranges, and chop them into roughly inch-square bits, or slice the apple into quarter-inch-thick slices. Allow these to dry, then sprinkle your choice of essential oil on them and place in a covered container. Open the container and stir daily until the peels or apple have absorbed the oils.

As a rule, use a half-cup of herbal blend to two cups of water. Place both in a saucepan on the stove, and gently simmer over low heat. Check it every quarter hour or so to make sure the water doesn't evaporate. Simply add more water as desired.

You can reuse simmering potpourri; simply drain the water from the pot and spread the plant matter out on a tea towel to dry, or line a strainer with a tea towel and strain the contents of the pot into it, allowing the plant matter to dry there (spread it out as far as possible and stir it once or twice a day to keep the air circulating and aid in the drying process). Be aware that the plant matter may stain the towel, so use an old one or one made of dark-colored fabric. When the potpourri is dry, place it in a bowl or jar to be used the next time. Mark the container with the blend and its purpose. Potpourri that is made of powdered herbs, as you may have on your spice rack, cannot be dried and reused.

Alternatively, you can put the potpourri in a small muslin or unbleached cotton sachet and slip it into the water like an oversized tea bag, or use a pouch-style tea bag designed for home blends. You can even place the potpourri on a square of doubled cheesecloth, draw the corners up and gather the cheesecloth together around the plant matter, and tie it closed with plain kitchen string.

There are special potpourri-warming pots designed for simmering potpourri that resemble deep cups with a partially open chamber beneath for a candle, or that run on electric power like mini Crockpots. These are unnecessary if your kitchen is central enough to serve as the staging-point for the scent infusion, but if you're looking to use simmering potpourri in a room far away from your kitchen then you may wish to look into these. Use sensible safety precautions with these devices, and keep a close eye on the water level. Keep them very clean, too, to avoid flare-ups or cracking. If you have old-fashioned radiators, you can place a bowl on them instead and allow the heat of the water inside to warm the potpourri water. Be very careful if you use this open-bowl method and have children or pets.

Here's a simple simmering potpourri to use during the winter holiday season:

You will need:

+ 2 tablespoons cinnamon powder OR two large cinnamon sticks (three small)
+ 1 tablespoon ginger
+ 1 tablespoon whole cloves OR 1 teaspoon powdered cloves
+ 1 tablespoon ground allspice
+ 1 whole star anise blossom
+ *Optional:* dried lemon peel, dried orange peel
+ Two cups of water

1. In a saucepan, combine the water and spices.
2. Gently heat the water on the stovetop over low heat. (If your potpourri is composed mainly of powdered herbs, fish out the cinnamon sticks, star anise, and peels to dry them and reuse them at a later date; pour the rest of the water and powdered herbs out.)

Sprinkling Powders

Sprinkling powders are used to distribute the energy of an herb or herbal blend around an area. It can be left permanently (as in outside), or left for a specific period of time and then swept or vacuumed up (if the intent is to absorb negative or unwanted energy).

The easiest way to make a sprinkling powder is to completely powder a single or a blend of herbs, and sprinkle it where you wish the energy to work. If you prefer, you can powder the herb(s) and then mix them into a neutral carrier such as cornstarch or baking soda. (Using talc is not recommended, because it can cause problems if inhaled.) If you use fine sawdust as a base instead, the resulting powder can be burned as an incense on a charcoal tablet (make sure the sawdust you use is safe to burn; sawdust collected from a workshop will generally be of wood treated with chemicals that are unsafe to burn and inhale). I generally use cornstarch.

Here's another use for sprinkling powder: Rub a candle with oil (plain olive oil or a steeped oil of your own making), then roll it in a sprinkling powder to load up on energies associated with your offering/petition.

Loose Incense

Making loose purifying incense is discussed in Chapter 7. For reference, here's a set of basic instructions for making a loose herb- and resin-based incense to burn on a charcoal tablet. You can use any combination of resins and plant matter, so long as you know they're safe to inhale when burned.

You will need:

+ 1 part resin (combined or single resins)
+ 1 part dried plant matter
+ Mortar and pestle
+ Small bottle or jar with lid

1. Place the resin(s) in the mortar. Gently crush the resin into small chips with the pestle. Transfer it to the jar. If there is any residue left in the mortar, scrape it out gently and add it to the jar.

2. Place the dried plant matter in the mortar. Grind them into smaller pieces, and transfer to the jar.
3. Cap the jar and gently shake it to combine all the ingredients. Label with the ingredients and/or name, and date.

Incense Balls

Incense balls are a fun alternative to loose incense, and useful if you wish to include liquid ingredients in your incense. The basic ingredients are ground resins, powdered dry herbs, and a liquid (such as honey and/or wine). Easy to use, these little balls stay on the charcoal tablet, have little mess to clear away, and burn slowly to maintain a level, ongoing release of energy. They store well, too, and make good offerings at your shrine, even unburnt. The term "ball" itself can be misleading. In reality you will be making small chickpea- or bean-sized pellets. Anything larger will not burn properly.

Incense balls are burned on a charcoal tablet. Make sure you use charcoal marked for indoor use, often sold in religious or ethnic shops. Bamboo charcoal in particular is a good choice because it contains no saltpeter, and is available in Asian markets or Chinatown areas. Never use barbecue charcoal, as the fumes can be toxic when concentrated inside.

If you prefer to make combustible incense—incense that can burn on its own—you would have to include a combustible ingredient such as fine sawdust, and often another additive such as saltpeter (sodium nitrate or potassium nitrate) or ground charcoal, which contains saltpeter itself. Although I've done it I'm not a fan of making this kind of incense, because I find it difficult to adjust the proportions and burn it successfully. If you are interested in trying your hand at this kind of incense, Scott Cunningham has recipes and instructions in his classic book *The Complete Book of Incense, Oils, and Brews*.

The basic proportions for making incense balls are:

+ 1 cup loose incense blend (made of resins, woods, herbs, flowers)
+ ½ cup dried chopped fruit (such as raisins, fruit peel, currants, apricots)
+ 1 tablespoon honey
+ Drizzle of water or wine

Here is a list of suggested ingredients for incense balls. You don't have to use all of them; pick and choose from among those listed. Just remember to keep to a 1:1 proportion of resins to plant matter.

+ **Resins:** Myrrh, frankincense, benzoin, copal
+ **Herbs:** Orris root, lavender, sandalwood, rose petals, cedar, cinnamon, nutmeg, bay, clove, ginger, rosemary
+ **Binding liquids:** honey, raisins, wine, fruit such as apricots or currants
+ **Essential oils:** Optionally, you may wish to add a few drops of essential oil as well, either to enhance the scent of one of the herbs you are using or to complement them.

To make incense balls, you will need:

+ Resins, herbs, liquid, and oils in the proportions above
+ Small bowls to hold ingredients

- ✦ Eyedropper (for oils)
- ✦ Measuring spoons and/or cups
- ✦ Jar or bottle with lid
- ✦ Waxed paper-lined tray or baking sheet
- ✦ Mortar and pestle
- ✦ Chopstick
- ✦ Rubber gloves

1. Crush the resins in the mortar with the pestle, or grind them in a coffee grinder (kept for crafts only). They don't need to be powdered, only reduced to small chips. Remember, the heat from the friction of grinding them can melt the resin slightly and make them gummy. Empty the crushed resins into a mixing bowl.

2. Grind the dried plant matter into small pieces, and empty into the resin mixture. Stir with a chopstick to combine.

3. Mix in the chopped dried fruit. Drizzle the honey and wine over the mixture. Stir to combine. The mixture should begin to clump together. Try forming a small ball; if the mixture falls apart add more honey or wine to moisten the mixture a bit more, and test it again.

4. Put on the rubber gloves. Scoop up a bit of the mixture and form it into small pellets about the size of a chickpea or slightly larger. Set the balls on the waxed paper-lined tray to harden and leave to dry for at least ten days to two weeks. Transfer the balls to a covered jar. Label the jar with the ingredients and/or name and date.

It is very important to allow the incense balls to dry thoroughly once you have formed them. I don't mean overnight, either: these will have to dry for at least a week or two, depending on how much fruit or liquid you've used. Besides this need, aging the blend for a couple of weeks to a month allows the fragrances to meld properly. Aged incense always has a more complex and developed smell to it. Allow the balls to dry on a flat surface for a few days before transferring them to a closed jar to finish drying and to age. Putting wet balls in a jar can backfire, as the wet parts may grow mold or stick to one another and form one mass, making removing a single ball to burn difficult.

Here's a tip for making the task of crushing or powdering resins less of a challenge: freeze for a quarter of an hour before crushing them. This makes them easier to powder. It also reduces the possibility of the heat of the friction melting the resin and sticking to the mortar and pestle.

Sewing and Other Needlework

Needlework of any kind is a method of altering, changing, transforming, or reordering something, and as such makes an excellent basis for hearth-related magical work. Whether it's as simple as hemming new curtains or a tablecloth out of a rectangle of fabric, like any other craft sewing can enhance and deepen the energy of your home and spiritual hearth.

This section will not go into fancy needlework, but you will find here one simple sleep pillow craft. If you're interested in other crafts that include sewing or needlework among them, look up Dorothy Morrison's *Magical Needlework* or Willow Polson's *Witch Crafts* and *The Crafty Witch*.

Herbal Sleep Pillows

Part of caring for one's family and home is making sure people get enough sleep in order to be well rested and able to operate at peak efficiency. If you or your little ones are having trouble sleeping, make a tiny sleep pillow to tuck under your full-size pillow and encourage restful sleep. Dill and lavender are both associated with sleep.

I recommend using a thicker material, such as felt, otherwise the bits of dried dill can poke through the fabric. If you wish to use a particular thinner cloth, double it. The color or pattern are your choice, although I suggest a soft color instead of something vibrant or saturated.

You will need:

+ Rectangle of cloth approximately 5 by 7 inches
+ Needle and thread (a complementary or matching color thread)
+ 1 handful of dried dill
+ 1 handful of dried lavender
+ 1 teaspoon of dried powdered orris root
+ Small bowl
+ Straight pins

1. Fold the cloth in two, so that you have a smaller rectangle. If you are using a fabric with a right and wrong side, fold the right

sides together. Sew along two of the open sides with a running stitch to create a pocket-like shape. Turn it inside-out so that the seams are inside.

2. Combine the dill, the lavender, and the orris root powder in the bowl, and stir with your fingers to blend evenly.

3. Pour the herbal mixture into the pocket.

4. Fold the raw edges of the open side inside toward the herbal mixture. Pin the seam and sew it shut.

5. Tuck the pillow under the regular pillow, inside the pillowcase of the full-size pillow. If it is for a young child, place the pillow on a shelf or hang it on a hook or nail on the wall by the bed, making sure it is out of physical reach.

Spell Bottles

A spell bottle is a collection of items with similar energy, brought together in one place for a specific purpose. Also called witch bottles, they're generally used for protection, but you can choose whatever theme you like. The bottle can be as temporary or permanent as you require. If permanent, you may wish to make it as attractive as possible in order to facilitate display on your shrine or the room it's designed to work in. You can even paint it a solid color, or paint abstract designs on it.

The basic technique for spell bottles is simple. In a jar or bottle of any size appropriate to your purpose, add:

+ Herbs that support your goal
+ Stones that support your goal

* Coins
* Symbols (small figures made of clay, or drawn on paper)
* Writing on paper (rolled up and tied with silk or cotton thread of an appropriate color)

Close the lid firmly, seal it with wax, if you wish, dripped from a candle. If you intend to keep the bottle in the home, decorate the bottle as you desire with decoupage, collage, painted symbols on the outside (runes, spiritual symbols, seals, or whatever you choose). You can varnish the bottle afterwards to seal your art.

Some older recipes for spell bottles include pouring a liquid such as water or oil (for blessing or protective bottles), vinegar or even urine into the bottle (usually for banishing bottles). I don't recommend it if you're going to use the bottle inside or for display, but if you wish to add a liquid to a bottle you intend to bury, go ahead.

Spell Bottle Variation

If the spell bottle is to be permanent, or a protective or enhancing talisman of some kind, try this variation.

In a craft store, look for clear glass ornaments. These are usually round and sold before Christmas. The metal caps slip off. Paint the globe first; they are very delicate and if it breaks, you won't have lost all the careful work of filling it with your ingredients. Take the cap off and fill the glass globe with your chosen ingredients. As the opening is so very small, you'll have to grind your herbs, use small chips of stones, and add very small scrolls of paper if you use them. The glass is very thin and fragile, so be careful. Use a funnel if you like, or make one of a rolled-up piece of paper. Seal the cap on this version of a spell bottle with a drop or two of glue to avoid the cap slipping off and the globe falling. Do not overfill the globe, or it will be too heavy.

These make lovely things to hang in windows, and to give as gifts. They are especially suited to charms and talismans for abundance, peace, happiness, and health.

Spoken Magic

There is power in words. A spoken word moves air, and creates the physical effect of sound waves hitting eardrum. In this way spoken words bring ideas from the mental realm into the physical world, an excellent example of manifesting your will.

An *incantation* is a fancy word for a spoken piece of magic, or the words that accompany a magical act. Other forms are charms, prayers, hymns, and so forth. "Magic words" are used in almost every culture's form of magic and also in worship.

Incorporating spoken magic into a daily spiritual practice isn't difficult at all. Spoken magic is a very common kind of practice. Think of saying "Rain, rain, go away, come again another day, [name] wants to play", or "Star light, star bright" when first seeing a star. This kind of folk wisdom, speaking things in response to an event or occurrence, is rarely seen as a kind of magic. More often it's seen as averting bad fortune in some way, or simply habit.

Also known as "country sayings" or children's rhymes, or even superstition, these bits of folk wisdom are sometimes rooted in actual historical events (such as the "Rain, rain" rhyme, which dates from Elizabethan times, and is believed to have arisen from the storm during which the Spanish Armada was turned back from England's shores). They are also often fortune-telling in some way, such as the "One for sorrow, two for joy" rhyme that can be applied to the number of crows or ravens seen in a flock, or even to sneezes. Alexander Carmichael's *Carmina Gadelica* is a collection of such prayers, blessings, charms, and incantations from the Highlands of Scotland, gathered between 1855 and 1910.

Spoken magic is one of the easiest ways to incorporate spiritual or magical practice into your everyday routine. Choose certain times or events and compose short sayings to speak when they occur, or certain spoken words to say when certain situations arise.

Doing so offers you an opportunity to consciously reconnect with the spirituality of the day.

Keep your sayings and incantations simple. When you look at traditional sayings they often have a beat or rhythm to them. Doing this with your own sayings facilitates the mnemonic. They don't absolutely need to rhyme, but a regular rhythm or beat does help. Keep the phrases short, so that you won't lose the rhythm of what you're doing, and so they're easier to speak and remember. You don't have to declaim them; murmuring them or whispering them under your breath is fine.

Here is a list of suggested times or events to initiate spoken magic. You don't have to use them all; these are suggestions only. Find a few that work for you.

+ Turning on a stone element or oven
+ Adding salt to a pot
+ Stirring a pot

- Setting the table
- Serving food
- Sitting down to a meal (yes, grace!)
- Opening the kitchen door
- Sweeping
- Washing the dishes
- Wiping the counter
- Turning off the light at the end of the day

Here are some examples of phrases to help you create your own sayings.

- **While stirring a pot:** "May my life be as cared for as my cooking."
- **While serving food:** "May the food about to be eaten nourish my family in both body and soul."
- **While sweeping:** "May all negative and nonsupportive energy be removed from this place."
- **When turning off the kitchen light at night:** "Bless this kitchen, and keep those of us who use it safe and in health through the night."
- **When opening the kitchen door:** "May only health, love, and joy come through this door into this house."

Traditional incantations and charms tend to invoke a deity of some kind. As this book is not specifically linked to any one deity in any particular spiritual or religious practice, there are no deity-linked sayings included here. However, people often like to link their sayings to their deity of choice, and I encourage you to do the same if you feel drawn to doing so. It can be as simple as saying, "In the name of [deity]" before the rest of the incantation.

Corn Husk Doll

A craft often done around the first harvest festival at the beginning of August (Lammas or Lughnassadh) is making a corn husk doll. Sometimes these dolls are used as the kitchen witch icons and hung in the window or above the stove for good luck. If you wish to make one of these corn husk dolls yearly, you can burn or compost the old one that has watched over your kitchen throughout the previous year. Save your corn husks when you eat fresh corn in the late summer; lay them flat on a piece of newspaper for a couple of days, then collect them in a paper bag and store them somewhere cool and dry like the garage. To use, lay them in a shallow pan of water to soften them up a bit. Soaking the husks helps make them pliable, so they don't snap when you bend them. They don't need to be soaked for long; five to ten minutes should do it. These husks can also substitute for wheat stalks in many crafts, if you cut or tear them into narrower widths. I use them to weave Brigid's Crosses at Imbolc. Just be aware they're a lot thinner and more bendable than wheat straws.

You will need:

+ Between 15 and 20 pieces of yarn for hair, each about 12 inches long (color your choice)

- Dried corn husks soaked in water (trim to approximately 12 inches long)
- Natural-colored cotton string
- Scissors
- Tea towel or clean cloth
- 1 twig, about 5 to 6 inches long and approximately ¼ inch in diameter

1. Gather the pieces of yarn and knot them together at one end. Take the husks out of the water they have been soaked in and pat the excess water off with the cloth.
2. Stack four husks on top of one another, aligning the long and short edges. Lay the yarn along the top of the husks, with the knot near the narrow end. Roll the layered husks around the yarn and tie the roll just above the knot with a piece of string. Tie it tightly, but not so tightly that it cracks the husks. Trim the ends of the string.
3. Fold the husks down over the knot to make the witch's head. Tie another piece of string around the husks at the neck. The yarn for the hair will now be revealed.
4. To make arms, roll a husk up tightly and tie a piece of string around the middle to keep it rolled. Slide the arm piece between the layers of folded-down husks. If you like you can tear the body husks a bit to place the arms where you want them. Trim the arms to the desired length and tie off each wrist area with a short piece of string.
5. Make the waist by tying a piece of string just below the arms.

6. To make a broom, cut an inch-long piece from the wide end of a husk. Cut a fringe in this piece by snipping a series of lines into it, leaving a solid strip about a quarter-inch deep. With the fringed end down, roll the strip around the end of the twig and tie it with a piece of string. Secure the broom to one of the hands by tying it with a piece of string.

You can refer to Scott Cunningham's *Spell Crafts* for other good crafts such as the creation of a corn mother figure, a variation on the corn dolly that creates a linked set of three circles of wheat, and a prosperity trivet craft.

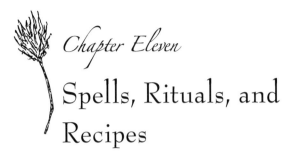

Chapter Eleven

Spells, Rituals, and Recipes

This chapter is a collection of home and hearth-based spells and rituals, most of them using the symbols of the cauldron and the sacred flame in some way. Purifications and cleansings are also a main focus here, as a lot of home-based spiritual work consists of keeping the home energy as clear and as positive as possible to support and nurture the people who live in it.

Remember, in the context of hearthcraft the word "ritual" simply means something set apart as conscious spiritual work and done with mindfulness, nothing complicated or confusing. While they're presented simply here, you can make these rituals as formal as you like.

Lighting the Oil Lamp or Candle

This prayer focuses on the use of a candle or oil lamp as a symbol of the presence of Spirit. Say it as you light a candle or lamp.

Sacred flame,
Burn brightly in my heart.
I light this flame in recognition of your sanctity.
Bless me, sacred flame,
With your light.

Consecrating Candles or Fuel

Hold your hands over the oil or candles and visualize the sacred flame represented by the hearth burning in your heart. Visualize the fire flowing from your heart to your arms and down to your hands. Visualize the light flowing from your hands to the candles or fuel, bathing them in the energy of the spiritual hearth. Say:

I dedicate these candles/this oil to the service of my spiritual hearth.

Cauldron-Based Spells and Rites

As the cauldron is a symbol of transformation, transmutation, wisdom, and abundance, it is easy to incorporate into hearth-based spiritual work. Rather than reiterate the ones already covered, the following will refresh your memory about the cauldron meditations and prayers in Chapter 4 and give you a couple to inspire you to create your own.

Simple Cauldron-Based Prosperity Rite

Put one penny in the cauldron every day, saying, "I invest myself in my spiritual hearth. Every day it yields abundance and calm to me."

Cauldron Harmony Spell

When your home has been a little less than calm, or if family members have been having a rough time outside the home, kick up the rest and renewal aspects of the spiritual hearth with this little spell. This one incorporates both the cauldron and the flame as symbols.

You will need:

+ Cauldron (small one is fine)
+ Kitty litter or sand (enough to fill the cauldron to the depth of about one and a half inches, or more if the candle is tall)
+ Pale blue candle
+ Matches or lighter

1. Pour a layer of kitty litter or sand in the bottom of the cauldron.
2. Place a pale blue candle in it. Light it, saying:

   My spiritual hearth is a place of rest and renewal.
   It nurtures me and those in my care.
   With this candle I invoke peace and harmony within this home.

3. Set the cauldron and candle on the physical analog of your spiritual hearth, or on your kitchen shrine.

Doorstep Cleansing

Here is an alternate and simpler ritual to cleanse your threshold or doorstep. It doesn't involve the extensive protection aspect that the ritual in Chapter 7 does, and as such makes an ideal method to use on a regular basis. Vinegar is a great negativity-buster, as is salt; cloves add a kick of purifying energy.

You will need:

- 1 cup of water
- 1 tablespoon of salt
- 1 tablespoon of vinegar
- 3 whole cloves
- Bowl or bucket
- Washing cloth

1. Combine the liquid, the salt, and the cloves in the container, and leave to steep in a sunny place for at least one hour.
2. Dip the cloth in the liquid and wash the threshold or doorstep. As you do, visualize any negativity clinging to it dissipating. Say:

   I hereby cleanse this threshold of negative energy.

3. Repeat regularly and as necessary.

House Blessing

This is a full-length, multistep ritual to bless your home. It's basic, and uses the four physical elements of earth, water, air, and fire to purify and bless the structure and the space. If you like you may follow this house blessing with the threshold protection ritual in Chapter 7.

You will need:

+ Cleaning supplies
+ Purification incense (see below)
+ Censer or heatproof bowl with sand
+ Charcoal tablet (if using loose incense)
+ Matches or lighter
+ Candle and candleholder (color your choice)
+ Small cup of water
+ Pinch of salt

1. Repair whatever needs to be repaired in the house. Thoroughly clean walls, floors, windows, cupboards, stairs, and so forth. As you do, move counter-clockwise through the house, finishing by sweeping dirt out the back door and shaking dust rags and emptying wash water out the back door as well.
2. Beginning at the physical analog of your spiritual hearth, light purification incense (such as the loose one in Chapter 7). Something like frankincense, sandalwood, or cedar would work well too if you prefer to use a purchased stick or cone.

3. Carry the incense clockwise through the house, going through each room. Don't forget to waft the smoke into cupboards and behind doors as well. As you do say:

With fir and air I bless this home.

Return to the hearth with the incense and replace it there.

4. Light the candle. Carry it clockwise through each room of the house as well, saying:

With light and flame I bless this house.

Return the candle to the hearth.

5. Take the cup of water and add a pinch of salt to it. Carry it clockwise through each room of the house again. Dip your finger in the salt water and touch the outside of each doorframe, then the inside, and the frame of each window and cupboard, saying:

With water and salt I bless this house.

If you prefer, rather than simply touching your finger to the frame or door you can draw a simple symbol that represents blessing to you. Return the water to the hearth.

6. Stand at your hearth and say:

Fire, water, air, and earth,
Bless my home and all those who dwell in it.

Room Blessing

This ritual focuses on a single room, and uses your associations with it as a basis for the blessing. As part of the blessing you will be creating a pouch to hang or place in the room. To prepare for this blessing, take some time to sit in the room you wish to bless and think about its identity. What color does the room's energy remind you of? Use this color to help key the blessing to the room. You can either choose ribbon of this color, or cloth of this color for the bundle you'll be making. If you choose to use ribbon of this color, use white cloth; if you choose a colored cloth, use white ribbon. You may use a candle that is white or your chosen color.

You can further tailor this blessing to the room by choosing different stones or colors for their energies that you wish to introduce or emphasize in the room.

You will need:

- Square of fabric 4 × 4 inches (white or colored; see above)
- Narrow ribbon approximately 10 inches long (white or colored; see above)
- 1 small amethyst or clear quartz
- Pinch of salt (for pouch)
- 1 penny
- Candle in candleholder (white or colored; see above)
- Small cup of water
- Pinch of salt (for water)
- Matches or lighter

1. Light the candle and place it in the center of the room. Say:

   By the light of this sacred flame,
   I bless this room.
   May it be a place of harmony.

2. Place the pinch of salt in the cup of water. Dip your finger in it and draw a line along the length of the threshold. Say:

   With this water and this salt,
   I bless the threshold of this room.
   May those who enter it know peace.

3. Take the square of cloth and place the stone, the pinch of salt, and the penny in it, saying:

   This stone for harmony,
   This salt for protection,
   This penny for abundance.

4. Gather up the corners of the cloth and tie it closed with the ribbon. Carefully pass the bundle above the flame of the candle, saying:

   I seal this blessing with fire.
   May this room always know light and love.

5. Hang the bundle above the door, or place it somewhere in the room where its energy can continue to bless it and say:

This room is blessed.

Personal Purification

This is a simple self-purification to do before an important act, or a good way to relax in the middle of something if you feel yourself beginning to get wound up, or if you're afraid or anxious about something. It makes a nice way to begin or end the day, too. It's particularly helpful when you want to focus on something if your mind is wandering or won't concentrate on whatever task you're trying to perform.

The candle you use can be one you light regularly in the kitchen as you work, or it can be one you keep for this particular purpose or for purifications in general. It does not need to be burned down completely. You don't need to use a lot of salt; a couple of spoonfuls is all you need.

You will need:

+ Small bowl or dish of salt
+ Small candle (color your choice; white is always good)
+ Matches or lighter

1. Place the bowl of salt on the table and sit down. Take the time to settle and fully feel yourself in the moment and mindful of your actions.

2. Take a few cleansing breaths and lift your hands. Place your fingers in the bowl of salt.

3. Close your eyes and breathe deeply. As you exhale, visualize any negative energy or the undesired emotion flowing down your arms and out through your fingers, being absorbed by the salt.

4. Continue to do this as long as it takes to clear yourself of the unwanted energy or emotion.

5. Remove your fingers from the salt and open your eyes. Focus on the candle burning on the table. Breathe in and as you do, visualize the warmth and brightness of the flame being drawn into your body, filling it with light and beauty.

6. Do this until you feel refreshed, focused, and calm. Extinguish the candle. Dispose of the salt by dissolving it in water and pouring it down the sink.

Creating Sacred Space

If you want to create sacred space in a more defined way for the purpose of a specific ritual or time for spiritual work, you can use this simple method. I've argued that the home is in itself sacred space, but there are times when we need to define an area that is set apart as particularly sacred for whatever reason. Think of this method as purifying a specific space so that it is immediately available for specific spiritual work.

Here's a simple way to create sacred space. If moving around the space you wish to define is difficult, you can turn in place and raise the element to the four cardinal directions, visualizing the energy of the element flowing out from the symbol in your hands and pushing away any unwanted energy.

You will need:

+ Candle in a candleholder
+ Incense and a censer
+ Small cup of water
+ Small dish of salt, sand, or earth
+ Matches or lighter

1. Light the candle and the incense. Take a minute to be fully mindful of the moment.
2. Carry the incense around the space in which you wish to work, saying:

   I bless this space with air.

3. Carry the candle around the space, saying:

   I bless this space with fire.

4. Carry the cup of water around the space, saying:

   I bless this space with water.

5. Carry the salt around the space, saying:

   I bless this space with earth.

6. Return to your starting place and close your eyes. Reach out with your heart and connect to your spiritual hearth. Say:

I call upon the power of the spiritual hearth to bless this space.

Sacred space doesn't have to be dismissed or undone in any way when you are finished. The energy of the surrounding environment will gradually flow through it and return it to its everyday status.

Various Recipes

Here's a collection of home-themed powders, oils, and incenses that can have various applications as you engage in spiritual activity in your home.

CARPET AND FLOOR PURIFYING POWDER

This powder features ingredients that clear negative energy as well as having the practical bonus of absorbing bad odors and refreshing your physical environment. You can also sprinkle it on fabric-covered furniture. It's nontoxic, so it's safe around pets.

You will need:

+ 1 cup baking soda
+ ½ cup salt
+ 2 tablespoons mint
+ 1 tablespoon dried lemon peel

- ✦ 1 tablespoon lavender
- ✦ 1 tablespoon rosemary
- ✦ 1 teaspoon ground cloves

1. Grind the salt, mint, lavender, rosemary, and cloves with a mortar and pestle, or in a coffee grinder reserved for arts and crafts use.
2. Combine the resulting powder with the baking soda.
3. Sprinkle it over carpets and floors and allow it to rest for at least two hours, preferably overnight.
4. Vacuum or sweep it up. Discard the contents of the bag or dustpan outside.

Oil Blends

I haven't really addressed essential oils in this book, namely because they aren't necessarily something everyone has at home. If you like to work with them or would like to try, here are some recipes for home-themed blends. Oil blends require a base or carrier oil such as grapeseed, jojoba, or other light oil. In a pinch light olive oil is fine. If you're sensitive to a particular oil, don't use it; substitute something else.

Try the recipes that follow. Tweak them as necessary to reflect the results you're looking for. Put a few drops of a blend on a vacuum bag when you put it in the vacuum. It makes the air smell great after a vacuuming session! The oils can also be rubbed on candles, used as anointing oil on objects or doorframes and so forth, or even yourself if you're in need of a pick-me-up.

HEARTH OIL

This is a blend designed to represent the energy of an idealized hearth. It contains cinnamon oil, which can irritate, so be careful when blending it.

+ 1 drop cinnamon oil
+ 2 drops sandalwood oil
+ 4 drops lavender oil
+ 1 drop jasmine oil
+ 1 drop rose oil
+ 2 drops frankincense oil
+ 1 drop pine oil
+ 1 tablespoon carrier oil

1. Blend and bottle. Label with the ingredients and date.

CLEAN AND BRIGHT OIL

This oil has loads of cleansing energy. Add a few drops to the wash water when you're mopping the floor, or on a damp cloth when you wipe down the counters.

+ 5 drops lemon oil
+ 5 drops orange oil
+ 2 drops peppermint oil
+ 3 drops lavender oil
+ 1 tablespoon carrier oil

1. Blend and bottle. Label with the ingredients and date.

PURIFICATION OIL

Use this oil to anoint objects in need of purification, or use it to cleanse stones or items you've been using to help maintain or balance the energy of a room. You can also put a drop or two on your wrists when you perform the personal purification ritual (see p. 228).

+ 5 drops frankincense oil
+ 3 drops sandalwood oil
+ 2 drops lemon oil
+ 2 drops lavender oil
+ 2 drops rose oil
+ 1 tablespoon carrier oil

1. Blend and bottle. Label with the ingredients and date.

BLESSING OIL

Use this oil to anoint objects when you want to bring a bit of positive Divine or spiritual hearth energy to them. This blend can be used in place of plain oil for the hearth recognition ritual in Chapter 3.

+ 4 drops sandalwood oil
+ 4 drops rose oil
+ 4 drops frankincense oil
+ 1 tablespoon carrier oil

1. Blend and bottle. Label with the ingredients and date.

SEALING OIL

Use this oil to close off and protect areas or items. It's also used in the protection ritual of Chapter 7.

+ 1 tablespoon carrier oil
+ 3 pinches salt
+ 1 whole clove
+ 1 sage leaf

1. Combine all the ingredients in a bottle. Label with the ingredients, purpose, and date. Allow to sit in a sunny spot and infuse for at least nine days.
2. To use, dip your finger in the oil and draw line across or along the area you are sealing (around a doorframe or window frame, along a wall, across a threshold, etc.).

Incense Blends

Here are several recipes for various incense blends. Blend them according to the instructions in Chapter 7 (and repeated as reference in Chapter 10).

PURIFICATION

Here's an alternate recipe to create a loose purification incense. I deliberately haven't provided exact measurements because beyond the basic rule of thumb to balance one part of resin with one part dried plant matter, the proportions are up to you.

- Rosemary
- Sage
- Clove
- Frankincense resin
- Myrrh resin

1. Blend and bottle according to the directions in Chapter 7.

ANCESTOR INCENSE

Good for honoring the ancestors, or appealing to them for aid and support.

- Rosemary
- Sage
- Myrrh resin

1. Blend and bottle according to the directions in Chapter 7.

Postscript

Several times as I wrote this book, my thoughts moved faster than my fingers, and as a result *hearthfire* very often came out as *heartfire*. I wonder, at times, if my subconscious was trying to tell me something.

At its core, hearthcraft is about honoring the home as a spiritual entity and a sacred place. The tips and techniques I've discussed in this book aren't what make a hearth sacred; it's how you live in a home that defines its sanctity, its ongoing life as a positive spiritual influence on those who live in it and visit it. In the end, your home-based spirituality is what you make of it.

I hope this book has helped you explore how you think of your home as a sacred place, and has given you some ideas. It's by no means limited to what's in these pages, either; everyone's perception of the sacred is different, just as everyone's homes and practices are different. We seek and find sanctity and blessing in many different places. I wish you peace and joy on your path.

Appendix

Ingredients and Supplies

This is a brief list of the associated energies of herbs and kitchen supplies, to use for various spiritual and magical purposes. It is by no means exhaustive. If you're looking for a good reference book to help you explore the energies associated with stones and plants, *Cunningham's Encyclopedia of Magickal Herbs* and *Cunningham's Encyclopedia of Crystal, Gem, and Metal Magick* are good places to start.

Blessing: olive oil, salt, water

Protection: rosemary, salt, clove, angelica, bay, fennel, rue, sage

Joy: lavender, lemon, orange

Love: rose, basil, apple, cardamom, vanilla

Communication: lavender, basil, carnation

Purification: salt, fennel, rue, sage, lemon

Abundance: basil, allspice, cinnamon, fenugreek seed, mint

Energy and action: cinnamon, ginger, clove, chili peppers

Health: ginger, lemon, apple, fenugreek seed, angelica, coriander, sage, orange

Meditation: anise, frankincense, sandalwood

Purification: angelica, sage, clove, salt, baking soda, lemon, rose

Basic Color Reference List

If a theme or energy you're looking for isn't on this list, think about the topic and choose the color that your intuition prompts you to pick. This is a good rule of thumb when looking at any color reference list: everyone is different, and one person's red may be another person's blue.

Colors

Red: life, passion, action, energy, fire

Pink: affection, friendship, caring

Orange: success, speed, career, action, joy

Yellow: intellectual matters, communication

Light Green: healing, wishes

Dark Green: prosperity, money, nature

Light Blue: truth, spirituality, tranquility, peace

Dark Blue: healing, justice

Violet: mysticism, meditation, spirituality

Purple: occult power, spirituality

Black: protection, fertility, mystery, meditation, rebirth

Brown: stability, home, career

White: purity, psychic development, blessing

Gray: calm, spirit work, gentle closure, neutralizing energy or situations

Bibliography

Ariana. *House Magic: The Good Witch's Guide to Bringing Grace to Your Space.* Berkeley, CA: Conari Press, 2001.

Carmichael, Alexander. *Carmina Gadelica Volume One.* The Sacred Text Archive. *www.sacred-texts.com/neu/celt/cg1/index.htm* (Accessed November 23, 2007).

———. *Carmina Gadelica Volume Two.* The Sacred Text Archive. *www.sacred-texts.com/neu/celt/cg2/index.htm* (Accessed November 23, 2007).

Clines, David J. A. "Sacred Space, Holy Places and Suchlike." Reprinted in *On the Way to the Postmodern: Old Testament Essays 1967–1998, Volume 2* (Journal for the Study of the Old Testament Supplement Series 292; Sheffield: Sheffield Academic Press, 1998). *www.shef.ac.uk/bibs/DJACcurrres/Postmodern2/Sacred.html* (Accessed February 6, 2008).

Cunningham, Scott. *The Magical Household: Empower Your Home with Love, Protection, Health, and Happiness.* St. Paul, MN: Llewellyn Publications, 1990.

———. *Spell Crafts: Creating Magical Objects.* St. Paul, MN: Llewellyn Publications, 1999.

———. *The Complete Book of Incense, Oils, & Brews.* St. Paul, MN: Llewellyn Publications, 1989.

———. *Cunningham's Encyclopedia of Magickal Herbs.* Second edition. St. Paul, MN: Llewellyn Publications, 2000.

———. *Cunningham's Encyclopedia of Crystal, Gem, and Metal Magick.* St. Paul, MN: Llewellyn Publications, 1998.

Dixon-Kennedy, Mike. *Celtic Myth & Legend: An A–Z of People and Places.* London, England: Blandford, 1997.

Eliade, Mircea. *The Sacred and the Profane: The Nature of Religion.* Translated by Willard R. Trask. New York, NY: Harvest (Harcourt, Brace & World), 1959.

————. *Patterns in Comparative Religion*. Translated by Rosemary Sheed. New York, NY: Meridian (New American Library), 1963.

Encyclopedia of Shinto.
http://eos.kokugakuin.ac.jp/modules/xwords/entry.php?entryID=208 (Accessed February 22, 2008).

Frost, Seena B. *Soulcollage: An Intuitive Collage Process for Individuals and Groups*. Santa Cruz, CA: Hanford Mead Publishers, 2001.

Guirand, Felix (ed.). *New Larousse Encyclopedia of Mythology*. Second edition. Translated by Richard Aldington and Delano Ames. London, UK: Hamlyn Publishing Group, 1968.

Homer. *The Homeric Hymns*. Online Medieval & Classical Library.
http://omacl.org/Hesiod/hymns.html (Accessed February 11, 2008).

Ingrassia, Michele. "How the Kitchen Evolved," Newsday.com.
www.newsday.com/community/guide/lihistory/ny-historyhome-kitchen,0,2541588. story?coll=ny-lihistory-navigation (accessed January 7, 2008).

Kesten, Deborah. *Feeding the Body, Nourishing the Spirit: Essentials of Eating for Physical, Emotional, and Spiritual Well-Being*. Berkeley, CA: Conari Press, 1997.

Lawrence, Robert Means, MD. *The Magic of the Horse-Shoe with Other Folk-Lore Notes*. Boston, MA: Houghton Mifflin & Co., 1898. *www.sacred-texts.com/etc/mhs/ mhs00.htm* (Accessed February 8, 2008).

Lin, Derek. "Drink Water, Think of Source." *www.truetao.org/living/1999/199909. htm* (Accessed January 11, 2008).

Linn, Denise. *Sacred Space: Clearing and Enhancing the Energy of Your Home*. New York, NY: Ballantine Wellspring, 1995.

————. *Altars: Bringing Sacred Shrines Into Your Everyday Life*. New York, NY: Ballantine Wellspring, 1999.

McMann, Jean. *Altars and Icons: Sacred Spaces in Everyday Life*. San Francisco, CA: Chronicle Books, 1998.

Mickaharic, Draja. *Spiritual Cleansing: A Handbook of Psychic Protection*. York Beach, ME: Weiser Books, 1982.

Morrison, Dorothy. *Magical Needlework.* St. Paul, MN: Llewellyn Publications, 2002.

———. *Everyday Magic.* St. Paul, MN: Llewellyn Publications, 1998.

Murphy-Hiscock, Arin. *Power Spellcraft for Life.* Avon, MA: Provenance Press, 2005.

———. *The Way of the Green Witch.* Avon, MA: Provenance Press, 2006.

Oxford University Press. *Shorter Oxford English Dictionary.* Fifth edition. Oxford, UK: Oxford University Press, 2003.

Polson, Willow. *The Crafty Witch.* New York, NY: Citadel Press, 2007.

———. *Witch Crafts.* New York, NY: Citadel, 2002.

Rose, Carol. *Spirits, Fairies, Leprechauns, and Goblins: An Encyclopedia.* New York, NY: W.W. Norton & Company, 1996.

Ross, Alice. "What Is a Kitchen?" *Journal of Antiques and Collectables,* May 2003 issue. *www.journalofantiques.com/May03/hearthmay03.htm* (Accessed December 7, 2007).

Rubel, William. *The Magic of Fire: Hearth Cooking.* Berkley, CA: Ten Speed Press, 2002.

Telesco, Patricia. *A Kitchen Witch's Cookbook.* St.Paul, MN: Llewellyn Publications, 1996.

———. *Magick Made Easy.* Harper Collins, CA: 1999.

Thompson, Janet. *Magical Hearth: Home for the Modern Pagan.* York Beach, ME: Weiser, 1995.

Tresidor, Jack. *Dictionary of Symbols: An Illustrated Guide to Traditional Images, Icons, and Emblems.* San Francisco, CA: Chronicle Books, 1998.

Wylundt. *Wylundt's Book of Incense.* York Beach, ME: Weiser, 1996.

Index

Printed in Great Britain
by Amazon